THE MOMMY LIFE

THE MOMMY LIFE

AN UNSHAVEN, MILK-STAINED (BUT HOPEFUL) PEEK INTO THE REAL WORLD OF MOMMYHOOD

GINA McMILLEN

Adams Media

New York London Toronto Sydney New Delhi

Adams Media
An Imprint of Simon & Schuster, Inc.
100 Technology Center Drive
Stoughton, Massachusetts 02072

Copyright © 2022 by Gina McMillen.

First Adams Media hardcover edition April 2022

ADAMS MEDIA and colophon are trademarks of Simon & Schuster.

For information about special discounts for bulk purchases, please contact Simon & Schuster Special Sales at 1-866-506-1949 or business@simonandschuster.com.

The Simon & Schuster Speakers Bureau can bring authors to your live event. For more information or to book an event contact the Simon & Schuster Speakers Bureau at 1-866-248-3049 or visit our website at www.simonspeakers.com.

Interior layout by Sylvia McArdle
Illustrations by Gina McMillen

Manufactured in China

10 9 8 7 6 5 4 3 2 1

ISBN 978-1-5072-1567-8
ISBN 978-1-5072-1568-5 (ebook)

FOR LILY AND OWEN

CONTENTS

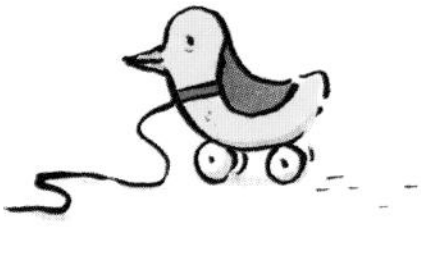

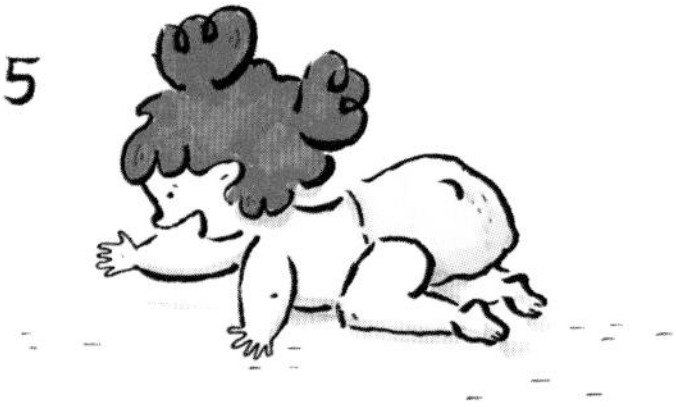

INTRODUCTION

Frantic middle-of-the-night web searches for "What does green poop mean???"

Patience-testing attempts to figure out which color bowl your toddler will actually eat out of.

An inability to get anywhere on time. Ever.

Parenthood can bring joy like nothing else—but it *does* have its fair share of frustrations too. Luckily, amidst all those sleep-deprived worries, endless diaper changes, and milk-stained sweats, are downright hilarious moments.

Before I had kids, I had a career as a teacher, hobbies, and a hearty appetite for good books. Then my daughter was born, and motherhood consumed me; I found myself a little lost. But one day in mid-2019, in an effort to find myself again, I scribbled my very first comic about daily life as a mom, and posted it to *Instagram*. It wasn't very funny, but for the first time since having children, it felt like the perfect blend between my old self and my new reality. What began as hastily drawn naptime doodles grew into a thriving creative practice and an amazing community of moms on social media. It turns out that I'm not the only parent who routinely loses her coffee cup somewhere around the house and hates cutting grapes into microscopic

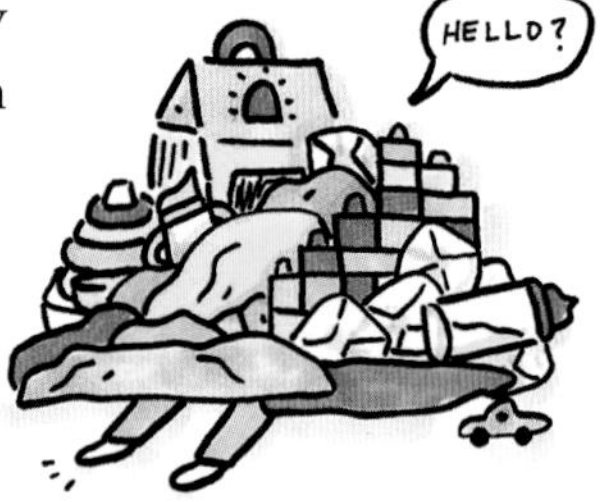
HELLO?

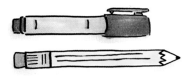

pieces. So many other parents online reminded me that I wasn't alone when I felt frustrated, panicked, or confused. Finding the humor in those difficult times is one way to help get yourself through them.

Whether you're looking for a laugh, a pick-me-up, or just a quick trip to the bathroom alone, *The Mommy Life* is here to help. The five parts in the book—New Mommyhood, Daily Life, Food Wars, Play Daze, and Me Time—include all the highlights of parenting little ones from newborn to age five. You'll find topics from diaper blowouts (*how* do they get poop on their necks?) and baby food (pro tip: stop feeling guilty about not making your own baby food, and use that baby blender for single-serving margaritas!) to first words (sure, "mugk" is close enough to "milk") and toddler toys (why do they never want to play with those lovely artisanal wooden options?).

Let these comics brighten the less-than-perfect moments and help you celebrate all the joy in between them…you know, like finishing last week's laundry before it's time to start *this* week's.

GINA MᶜMILLEN

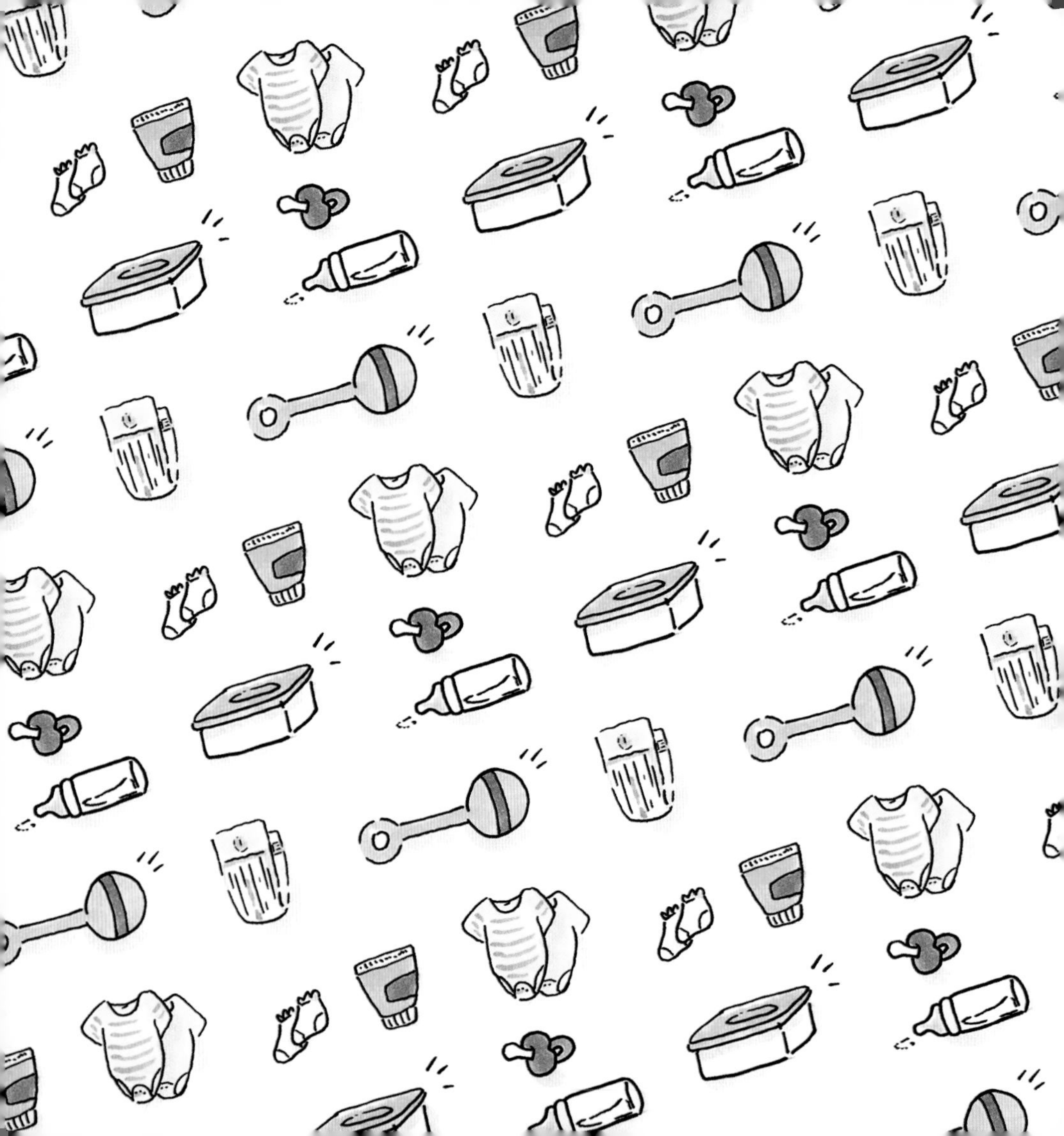

① NEW MOMMYHOOD

☑ BLOWOUTS

☑ BURPS

☑ BOOBS

MOM BATTERY

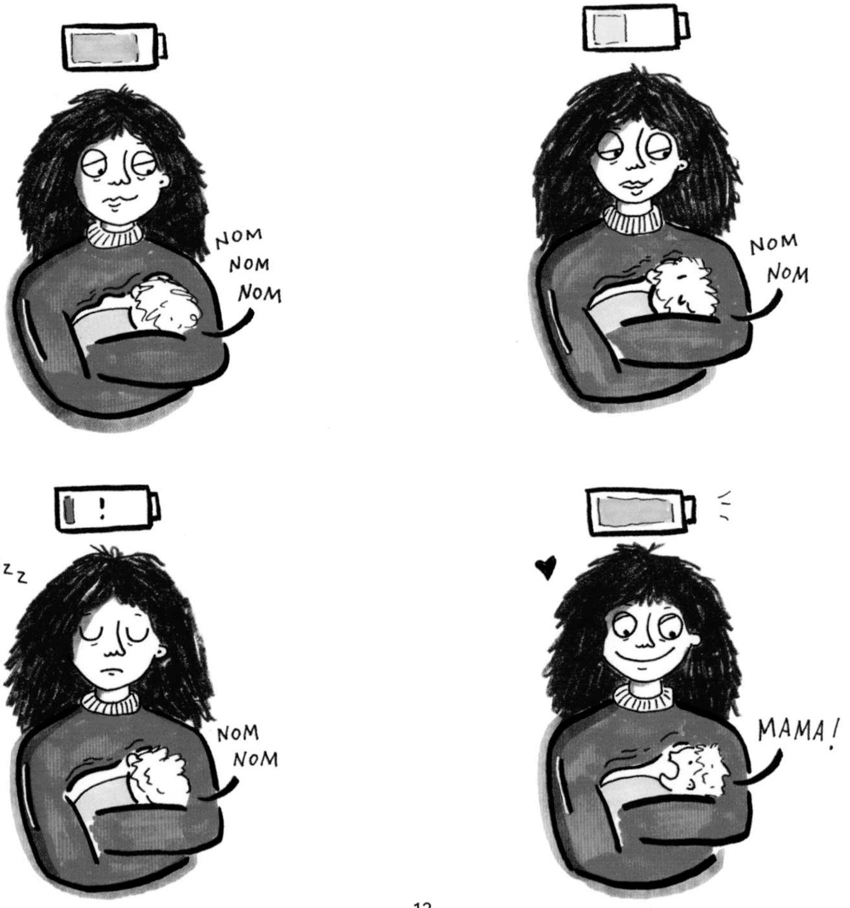

NOM
NOM
NOM
NOM
NOM
ZZZ
NOM
NOM
MAMA!

NEWBORN LIFE BE LIKE...

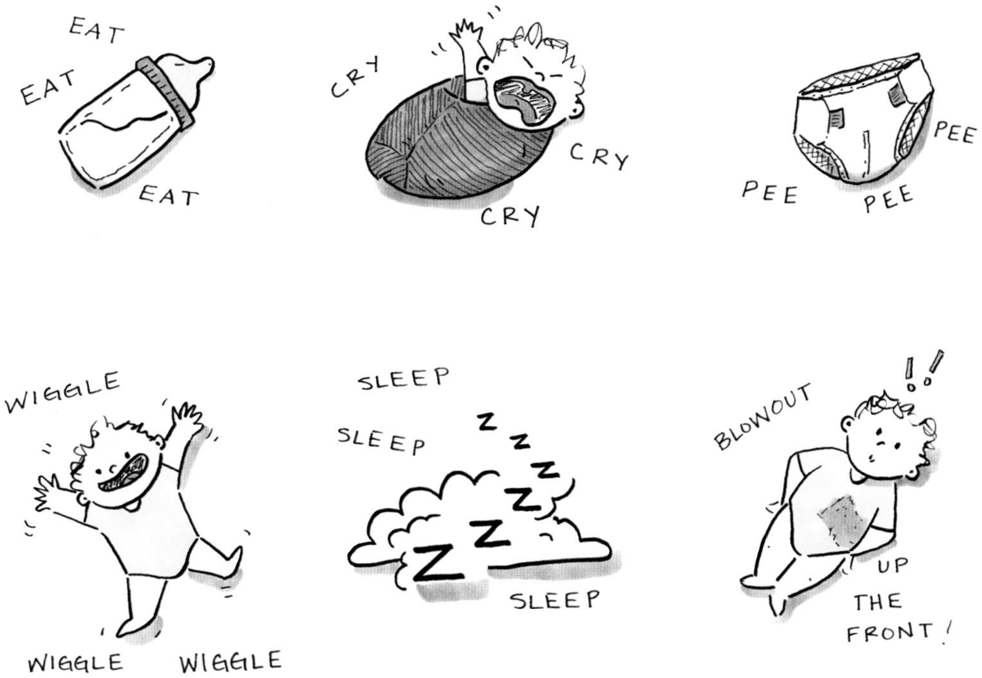
EAT
EAT
EAT
CRY
CRY
CRY
PEE
PEE
PEE
WIGGLE
WIGGLE
WIGGLE
SLEEP
SLEEP
SLEEP
BLOWOUT
!!
UP
THE
FRONT!

NEW MOM'S BOOKSHELF

BABY POOP IN PICTURES

EAT, SLEEP, POOP

A MEMOIR

MAKING COFFEE WITH ONE HAND

HOMEMADE DIAPER CREAMS

MUCUS PLUGS FOR DUMMIES

CHAPSTICK AND OTHER DUMB THINGS TO PACK IN YOUR HOSPITAL BAG *

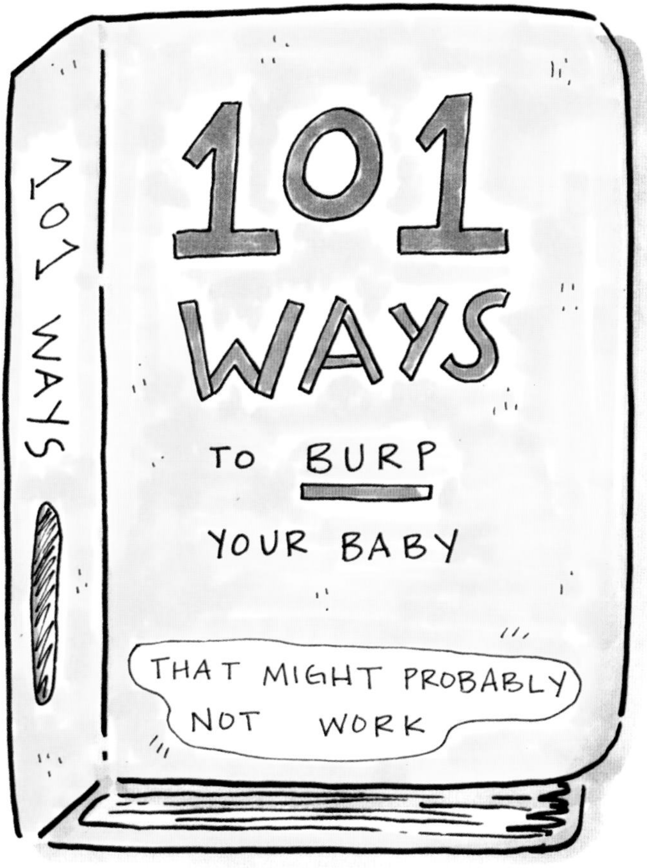
101 WAYS
101 WAYS
TO BURP YOUR BABY
THAT MIGHT PROBABLY NOT WORK

FEELING

~~PUMPED~~

~~DRAINED~~

~~SUCKY~~

LIKE A LIFE-
GIVING GODDESS.

PUMPING-AT-WORK ANXIETY

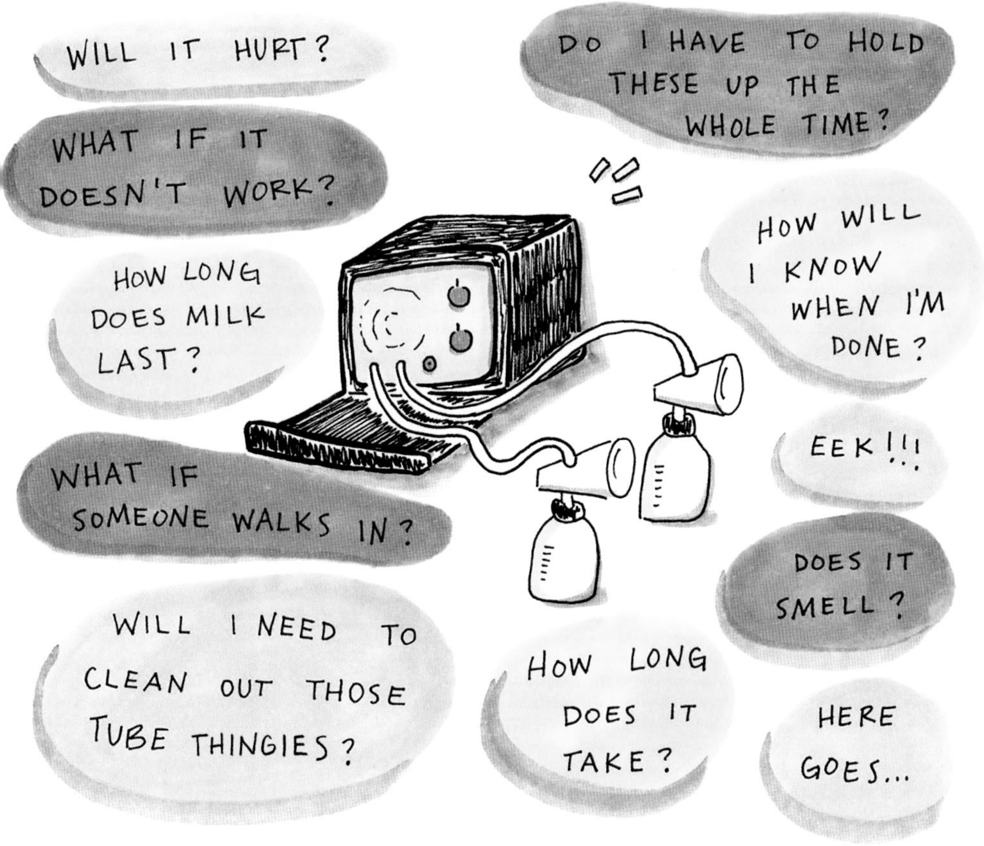
WILL IT HURT?
DO I HAVE TO HOLD THESE UP THE WHOLE TIME?
WHAT IF IT DOESN'T WORK?
HOW LONG DOES MILK LAST?
HOW WILL I KNOW WHEN I'M DONE?
EEK!!!
WHAT IF SOMEONE WALKS IN?
DOES IT SMELL?
WILL I NEED TO CLEAN OUT THOSE TUBE THINGIES?
HOW LONG DOES IT TAKE?
HERE GOES...

UNWANTED

THE BABY GIFT WE

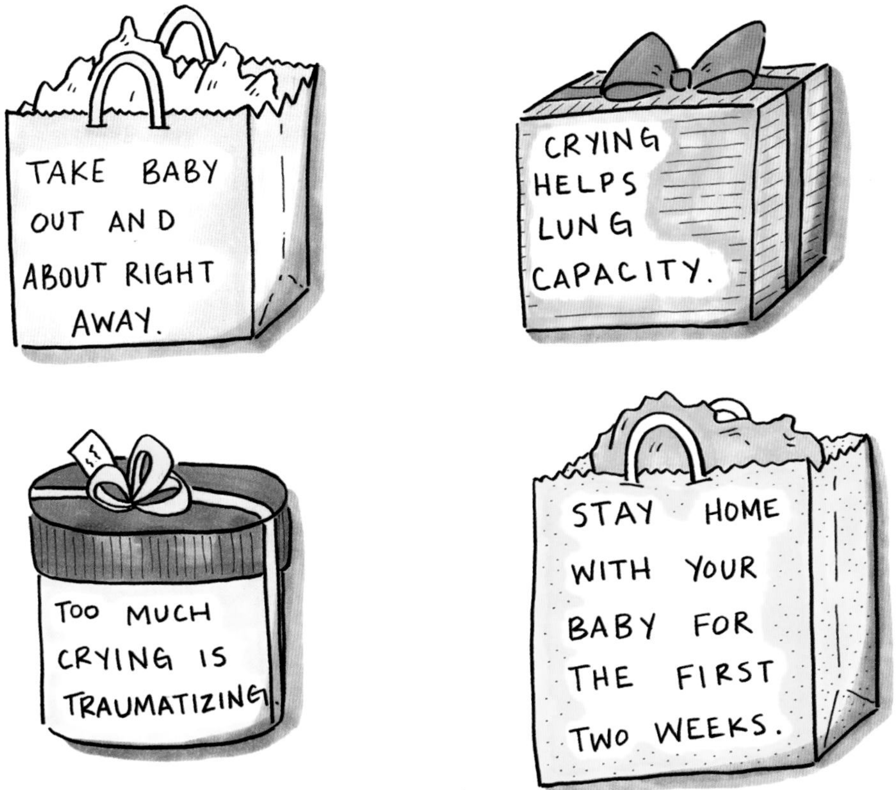
TAKE BABY OUT AND ABOUT RIGHT AWAY.
CRYING HELPS LUNG CAPACITY.
TOO MUCH CRYING IS TRAUMATIZING.
STAY HOME WITH YOUR BABY FOR THE FIRST TWO WEEKS.

ADVICE

NEVER REGISTERED FOR

REMEMBER "NO" IS A NAUGHTY WORD.

EXPOSE THE BABY TO ALL THE GERMS.

SLEEP WHEN BABY SLEEPS!

BABY'S "SECOND" FAVORITE TEETHER

BITE ME!

WHAT'S IN MY BAG:

DIAPER BAG EDITION *

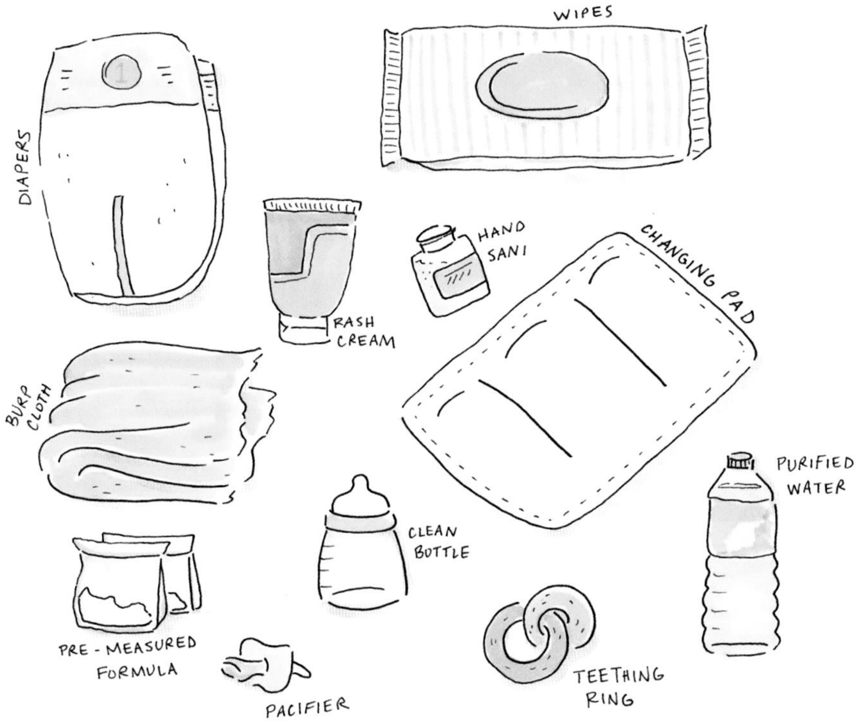
WIPES
DIAPERS
HAND SANI
CHANGING PAD
RASH CREAM
BURP CLOTH
PURIFIED WATER
CLEAN BOTTLE
PRE-MEASURED FORMULA
TEETHING RING
PACIFIER

* NOT PICTURED: A DOZEN EMERGENCY OUTFITS

THE SUGGESTED SNACK FOR A BREASTFEEDING MOM

A SMALL BOWL OF ALMONDS

MY ACTUAL SNACK

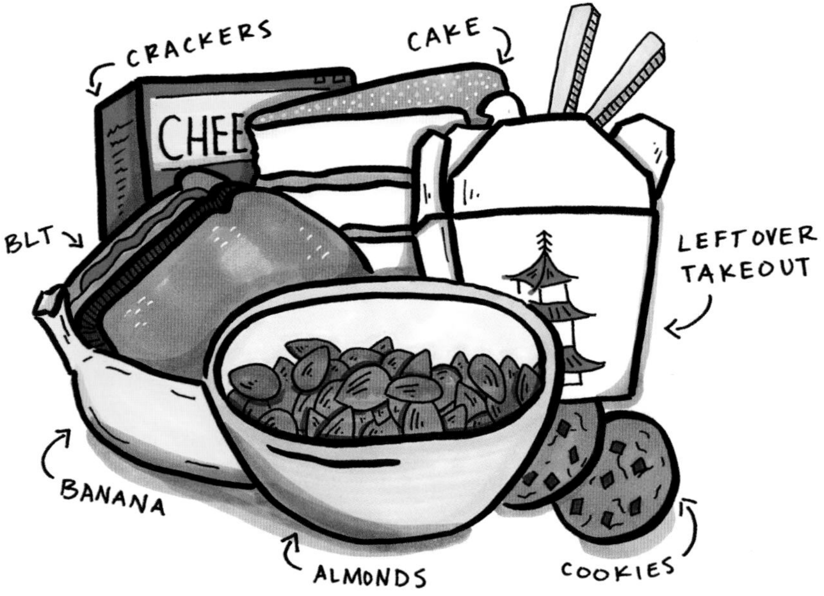

CRACKERS
CHEE
CAKE
BLT
LEFTOVER TAKEOUT
BANANA
ALMONDS
COOKIES

I
SPY
ON MY
BABY
EVERY NIGHT.

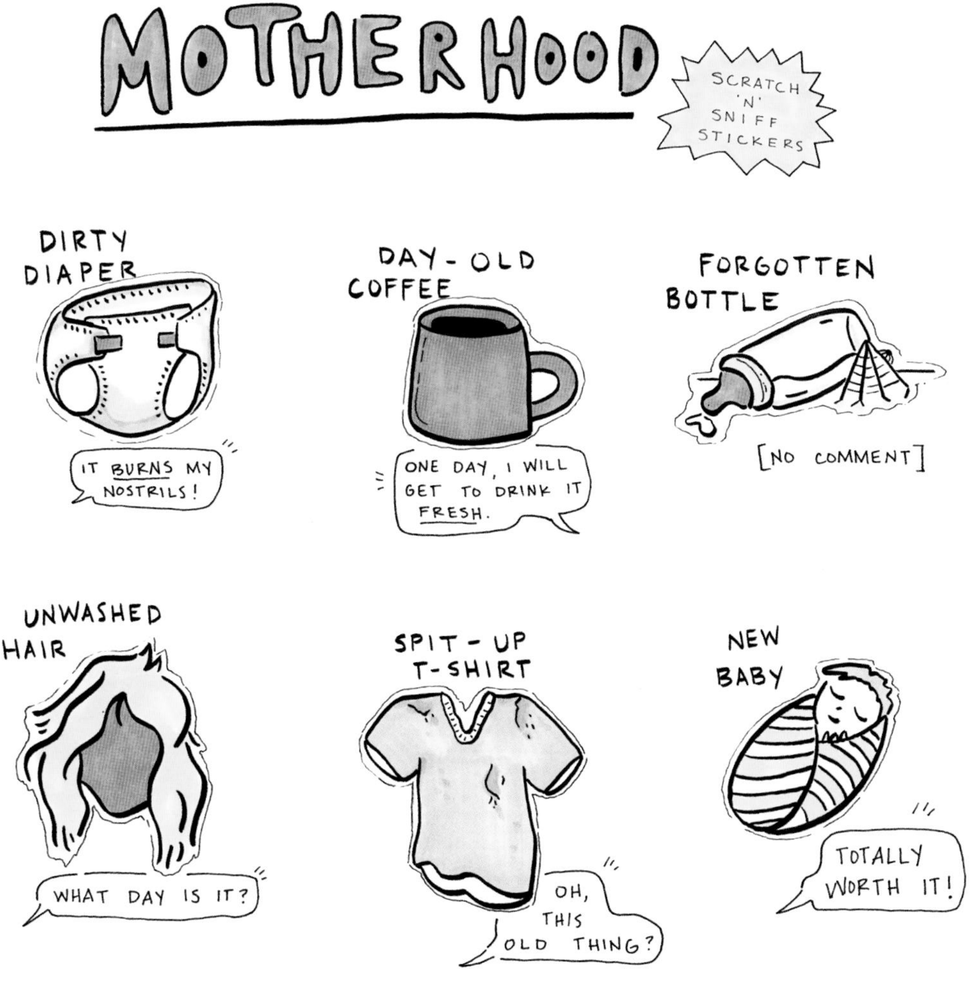
MOTHERHOOD
SCRATCH 'N' SNIFF STICKERS
DIRTY DIAPER
IT BURNS MY NOSTRILS!
DAY-OLD COFFEE
ONE DAY, I WILL GET TO DRINK IT FRESH.
FORGOTTEN BOTTLE
[NO COMMENT]
UNWASHED HAIR
WHAT DAY IS IT?
SPIT-UP T-SHIRT
OH, THIS OLD THING?
NEW BABY
TOTALLY WORTH IT!

MOMMY MESSAGE BOARDS

(A.K.A. THE PIT OF DESPAIR)

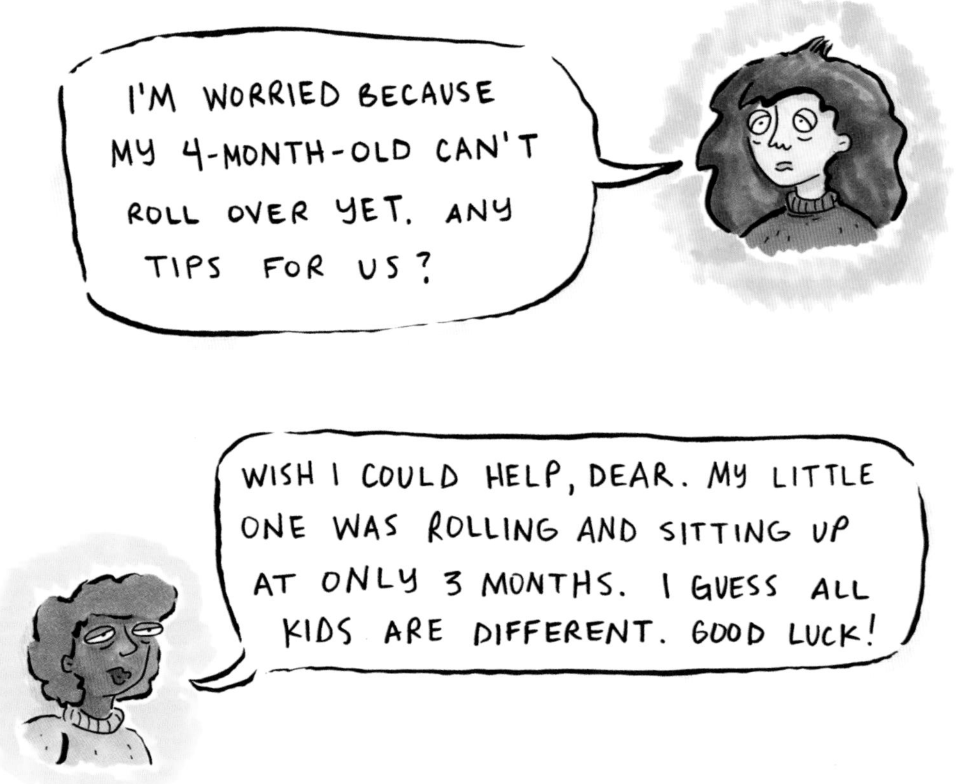
I'M WORRIED BECAUSE MY 4-MONTH-OLD CAN'T ROLL OVER YET. ANY TIPS FOR US?
WISH I COULD HELP, DEAR. MY LITTLE ONE WAS ROLLING AND SITTING UP AT ONLY 3 MONTHS. I GUESS ALL KIDS ARE DIFFERENT. GOOD LUCK!

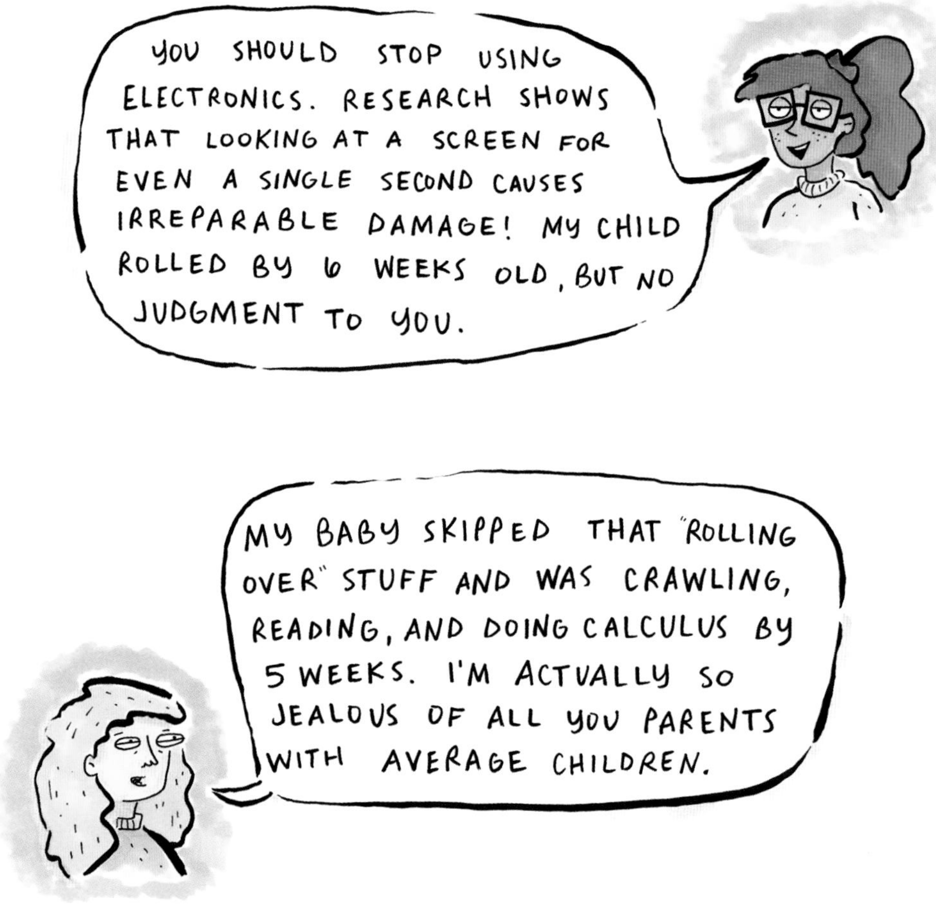
YOU SHOULD STOP USING ELECTRONICS. RESEARCH SHOWS THAT LOOKING AT A SCREEN FOR EVEN A SINGLE SECOND CAUSES IRREPARABLE DAMAGE! MY CHILD ROLLED BY 6 WEEKS OLD, BUT NO JUDGMENT TO YOU.
MY BABY SKIPPED THAT "ROLLING OVER" STUFF AND WAS CRAWLING, READING, AND DOING CALCULUS BY 5 WEEKS. I'M ACTUALLY SO JEALOUS OF ALL YOU PARENTS WITH AVERAGE CHILDREN.

WHAT SHALL I WEAR TODAY?

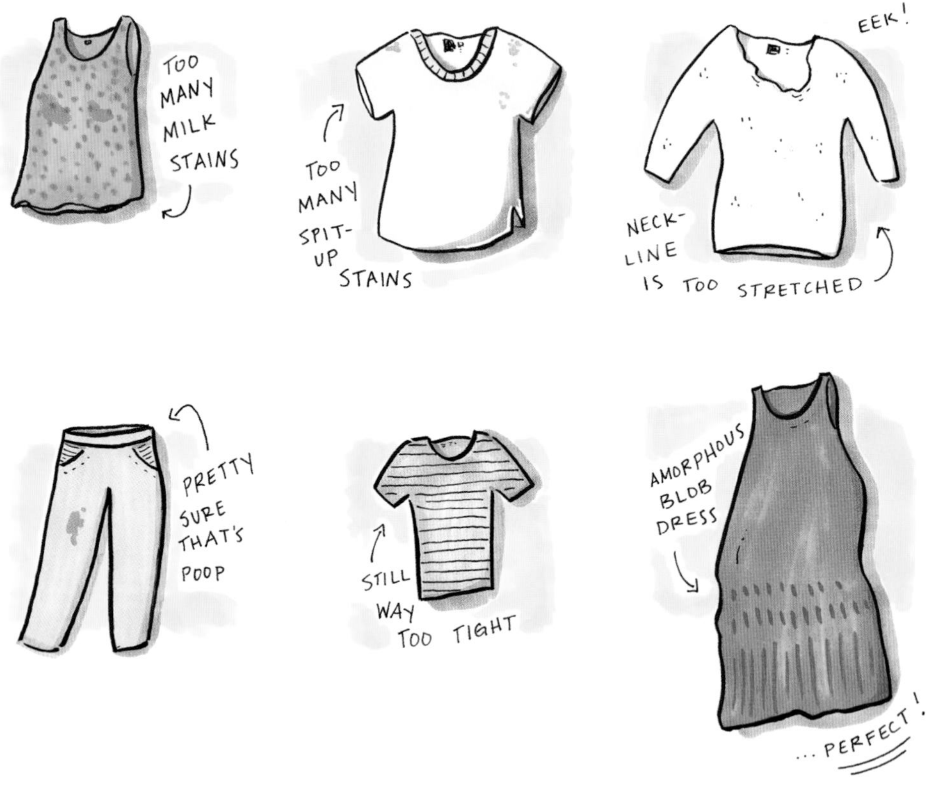
TOO MANY MILK STAINS
TOO MANY SPIT-UP STAINS
EEK!
NECK-LINE IS TOO STRETCHED
PRETTY SURE THAT'S POOP
STILL WAY TOO TIGHT
AMORPHOUS BLOB DRESS
... PERFECT!

I ^ACTUALLY NAPPED

WHEN BABY

NAPPED!

FOUR MONTHS LATER AND THANKFULLY "SOMEONE" SLEEPS IN THE CRIB.

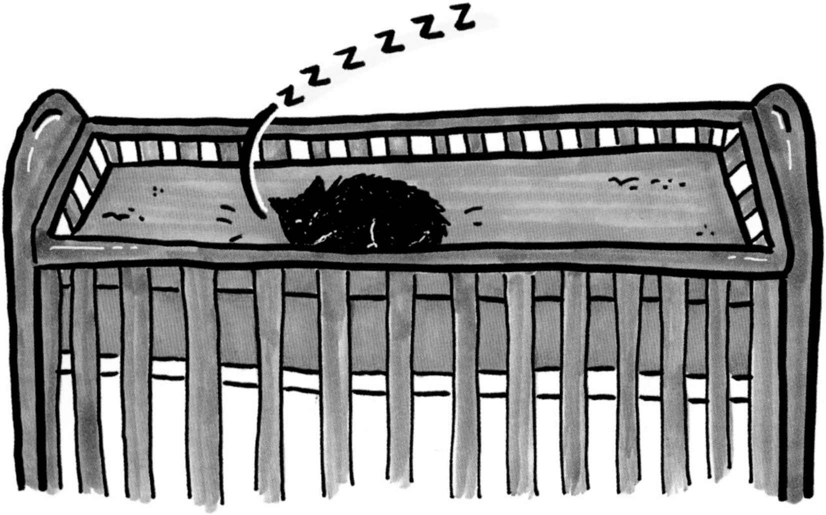
ZZZZZZZ

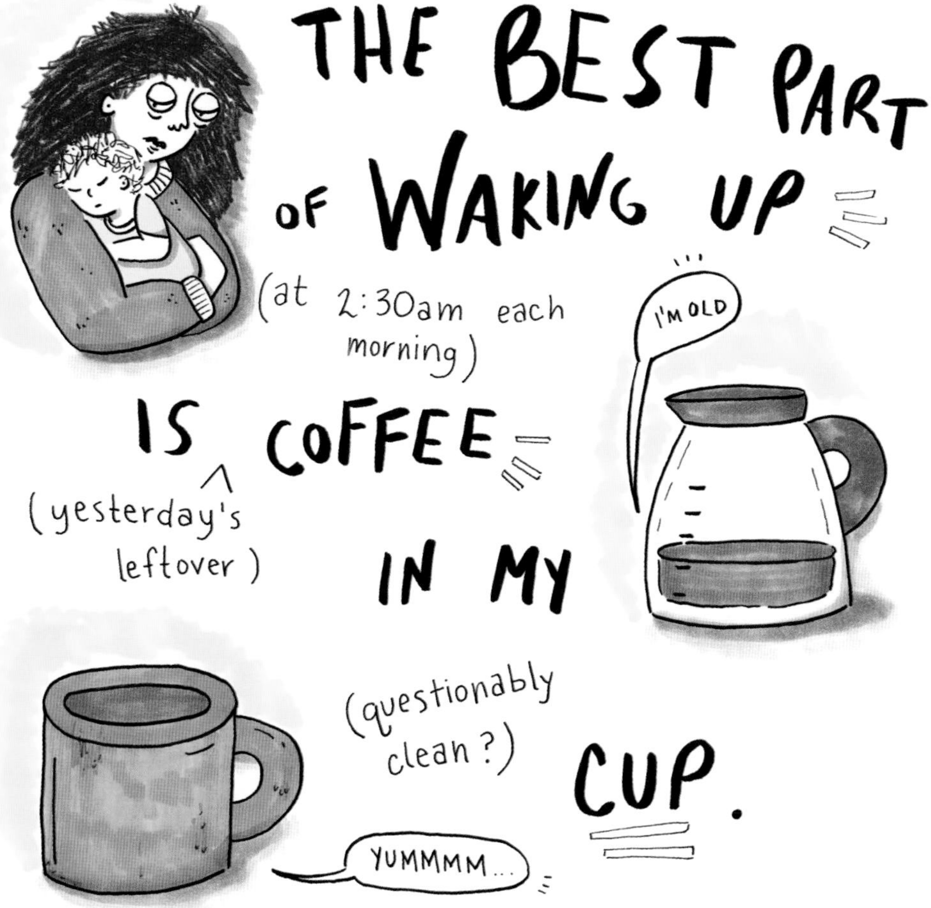
THE BEST PART
OF WAKING UP
(at 2:30am each morning)
IS (yesterday's leftover) COFFEE
I'M OLD
IN MY
(questionably clean?)
CUP.
YUMMMM...

I'D NAP ON THAT!

THE TOILET

THIS "QUESTIONABLE" COUCH AT A FRIEND'S HOUSE

THE GROCERY SHOPPING CART

THE STAIRS

MY EVER-
GROWING PILE
OF <u>LAUNDRY</u> —

A TUNNEL
SLIDE AT THE
PARK

I SMELL
LIKE
FEET

THAT
FLUFFY
SHOWROOM
RUG

THIS GUY ON
THE
BUS

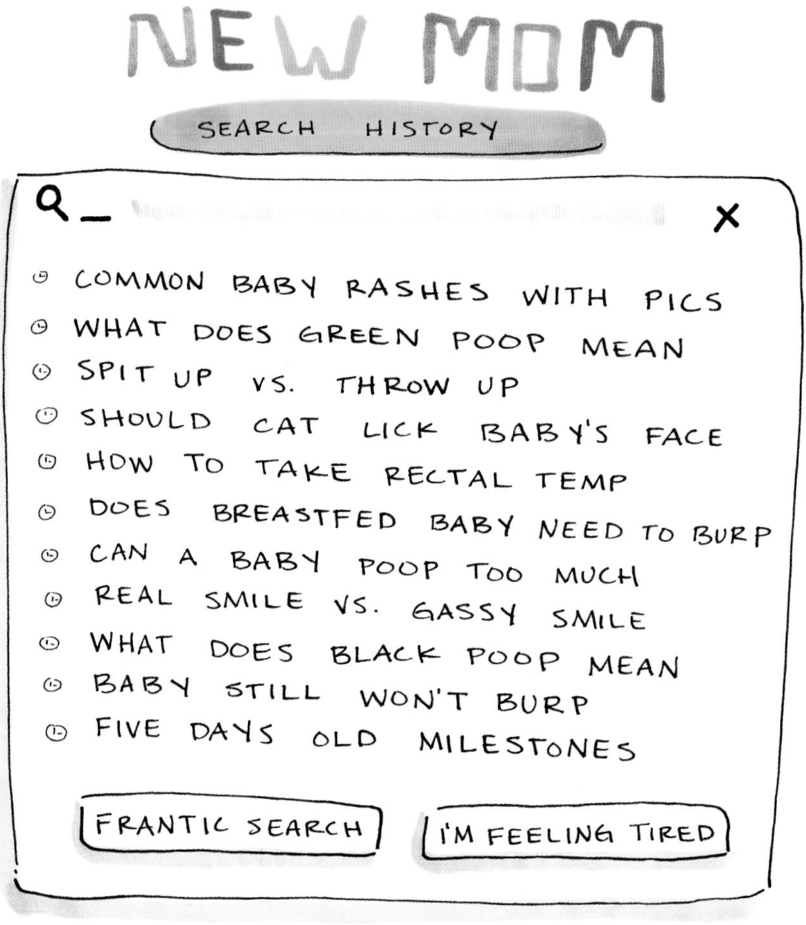
NEW MOM
SEARCH HISTORY
COMMON BABY RASHES WITH PICS
WHAT DOES GREEN POOP MEAN
SPIT UP VS. THROW UP
SHOULD CAT LICK BABY'S FACE
HOW TO TAKE RECTAL TEMP
DOES BREASTFED BABY NEED TO BURP
CAN A BABY POOP TOO MUCH
REAL SMILE VS. GASSY SMILE
WHAT DOES BLACK POOP MEAN
BABY STILL WON'T BURP
FIVE DAYS OLD MILESTONES
FRANTIC SEARCH
I'M FEELING TIRED

THE OTHER NEWBORN MILESTONES

FIRST BLOWOUT

SIDE BLOWOUT

BLOW-OUT IN THE CAR

NUCLEAR BLOWDUT

CRIME SCENE BLOWOUT

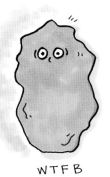

WTFB

FIRST CHILD'S WARDROBE

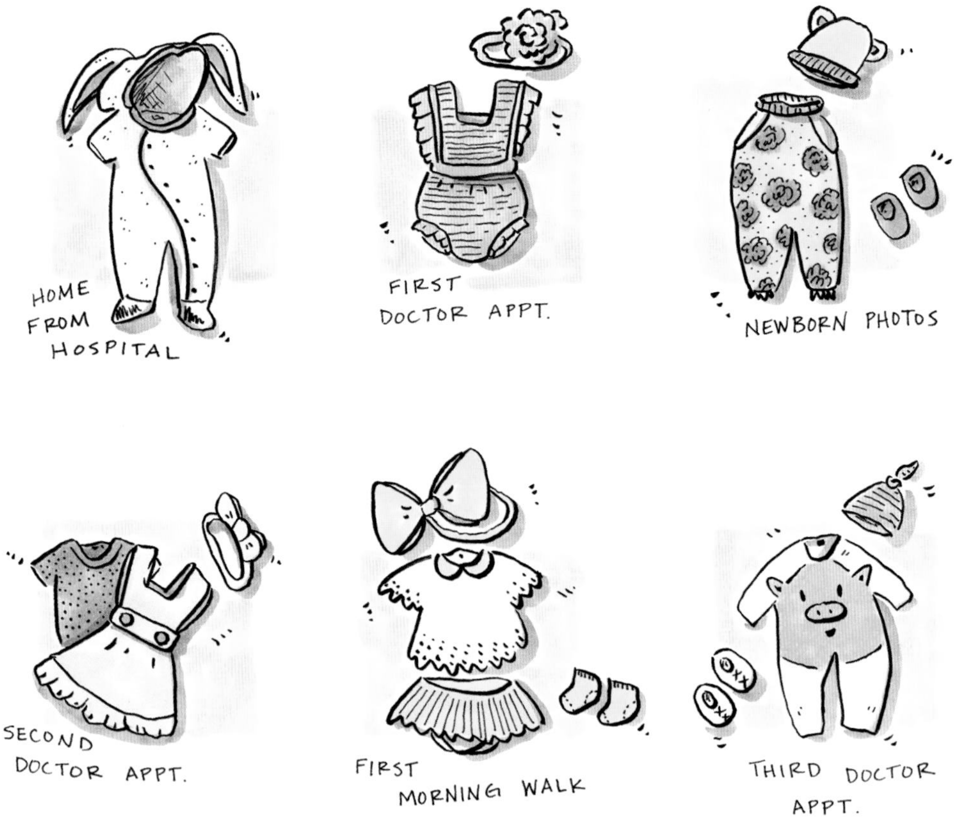
HOME FROM HOSPITAL
FIRST DOCTOR APPT.
NEWBORN PHOTOS
SECOND DOCTOR APPT.
FIRST MORNING WALK
THIRD DOCTOR APPT.

SECOND CHILD'S WARDROBE

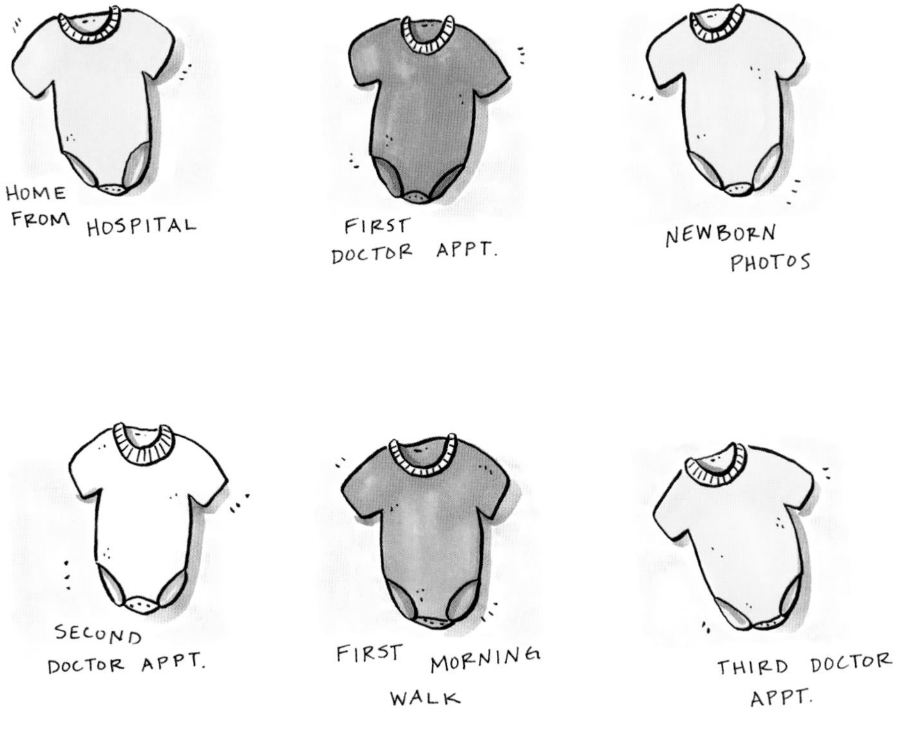
HOME FROM HOSPITAL
FIRST DOCTOR APPT.
NEWBORN PHOTOS
SECOND DOCTOR APPT.
FIRST MORNING WALK
THIRD DOCTOR APPT.

THE SELF-PORTRAIT

I NEVER EXPECTED

TO DRAW.

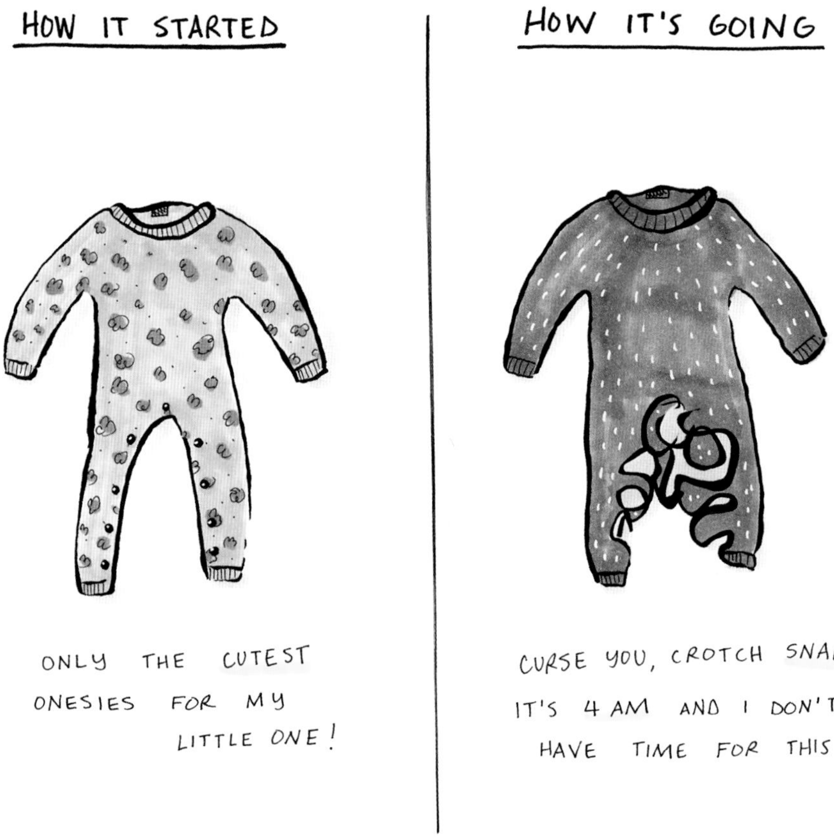
HOW IT STARTED
ONLY THE CUTEST ONESIES FOR MY LITTLE ONE!
HOW IT'S GOING
CURSE YOU, CROTCH SNAPS! IT'S 4 AM AND I DON'T HAVE TIME FOR THIS!

PROUD MOMMY AWARDS

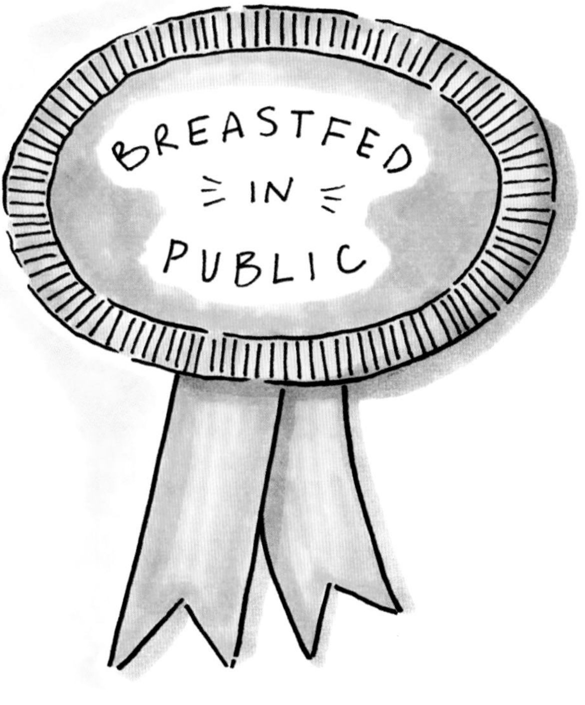
BREASTFED
IN
PUBLIC

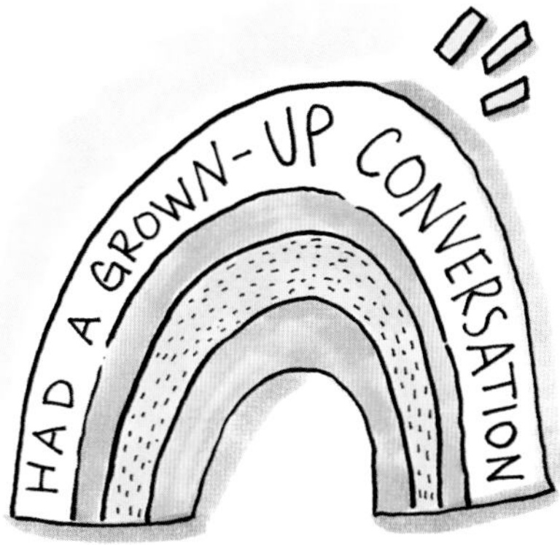
HAD A GROWN-UP CONVERSATION

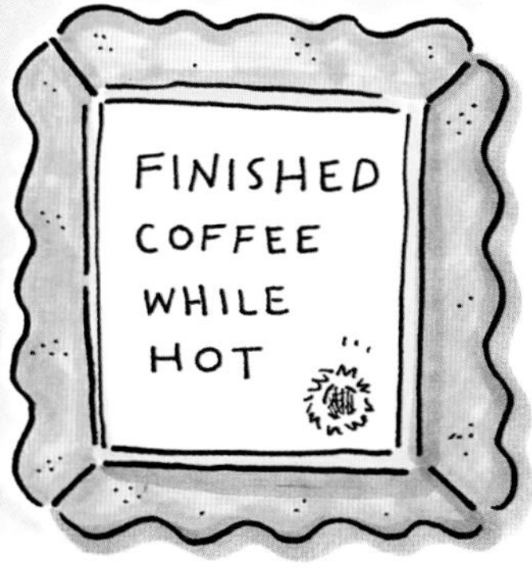
FINISHED COFFEE WHILE HOT

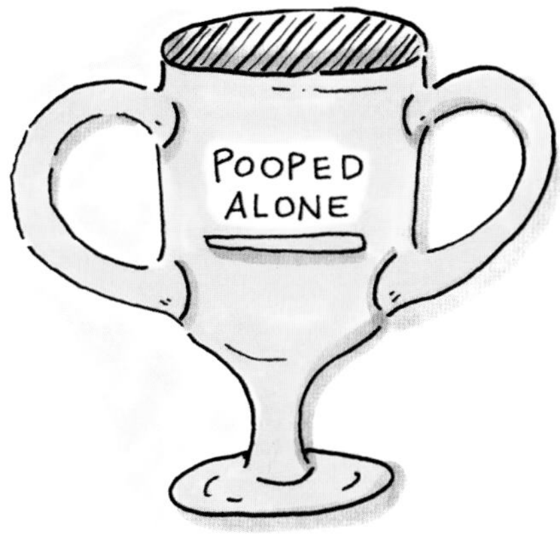
POOPED ALONE

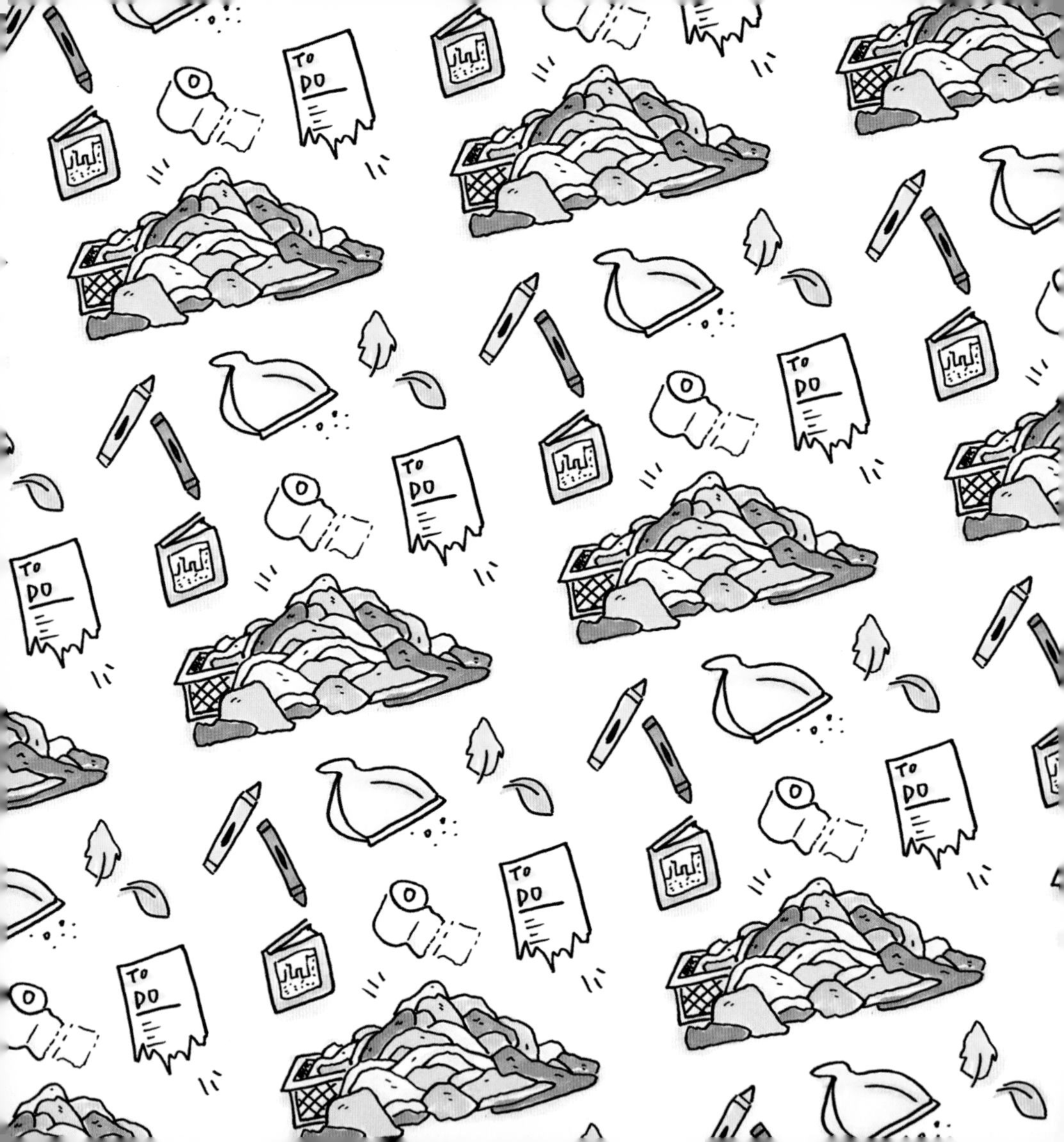
TO DO
TO DO
TO DO
TO DO
TO DO
TO DO
TO DO

2

DAILY LIFE

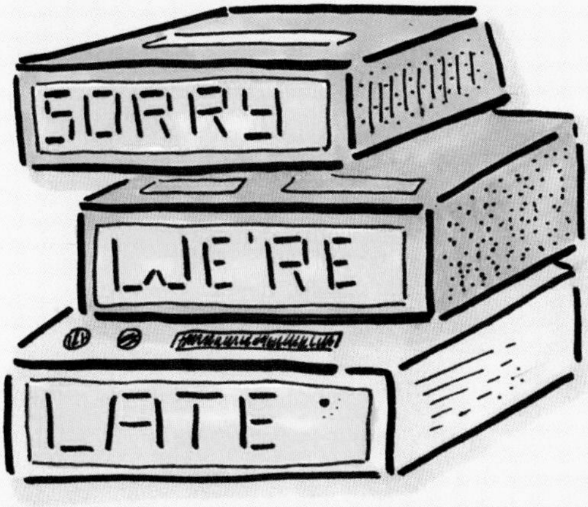
SORRY
WE'RE
LATE

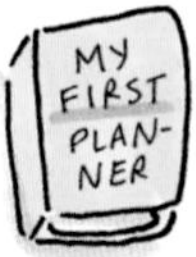
MY FIRST PLANNER

I FOUND MY TODDLER'S DAY PLANNER...
LOOKS LIKE SHE KEEPS A TIGHT SCHEDULE.

5:45 AM

- ☐ WAKE UP
- ☐ POOP MY PANTS
- ☐ GET MOMMY

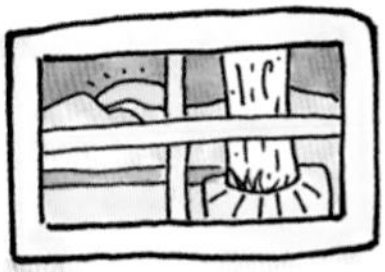

6:15AM

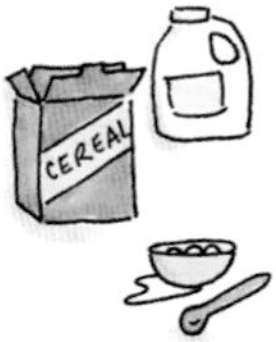
CEREAL

- ☐ GET DRESSED
- ☐ POUR MY OWN CEREAL
- ☐ SPILL MY OWN CEREAL
- ☐ CHANGE CLOTHES
- ☐ EAT MOMMY'S CEREAL

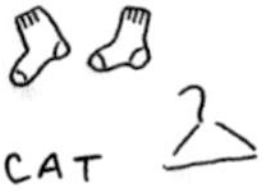

8:30 AM

- ☐ PLAY ONLY WITH THE BABY'S TOYS
- ☐ SAY "SNACK" 42 TIMES
- ☐ CHASE THE CAT
- ☐ EAT SNACK
- ☐ CHANGE MY CLOTHES AGAIN

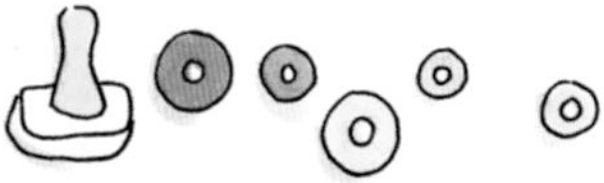

11:00 AM

- ☐ OUTSIDE TIME
- ☐ DECONSTRUCT LUNCH
- ☐ 25 MINUTE POOP
- ☐ JUST KIDDING IT WAS ONLY A PEE ☺
- ☐ NAPTIME TANTRUM

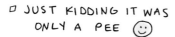

2:00 PM

- ☐ WAKE UP CRANKY
- ☐ SNACK !!!!!
  - ☐ WAKE UP BABY
- ☐ SPIN AROUND IN CIRCLES TILL I FALL DOWN

5:00 PM

- ☐ POKE DINNER
- ☐ JUMP ON THE COUCH
- ☐ JUMP ON THE BED
- ☐ JUMP IN THE BATH
- ☐ SHOW MOMMY MY AWESOME JUMPING SKILLS

LOOK IT!

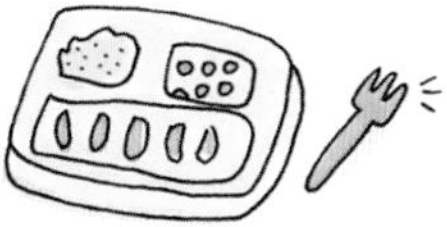

8:00 PM

- ☐ READ AT LEAST 3 BOOKS
- ☐ HUGS 'N' KISSES
- ☐ GOODNIGHT
- -> ☐ ASK FOR WATER
- ☐ GO TO BATHROOM
- ☐ 1 MORE STORY
- ☐ LIGHTS OUT

REPEAT

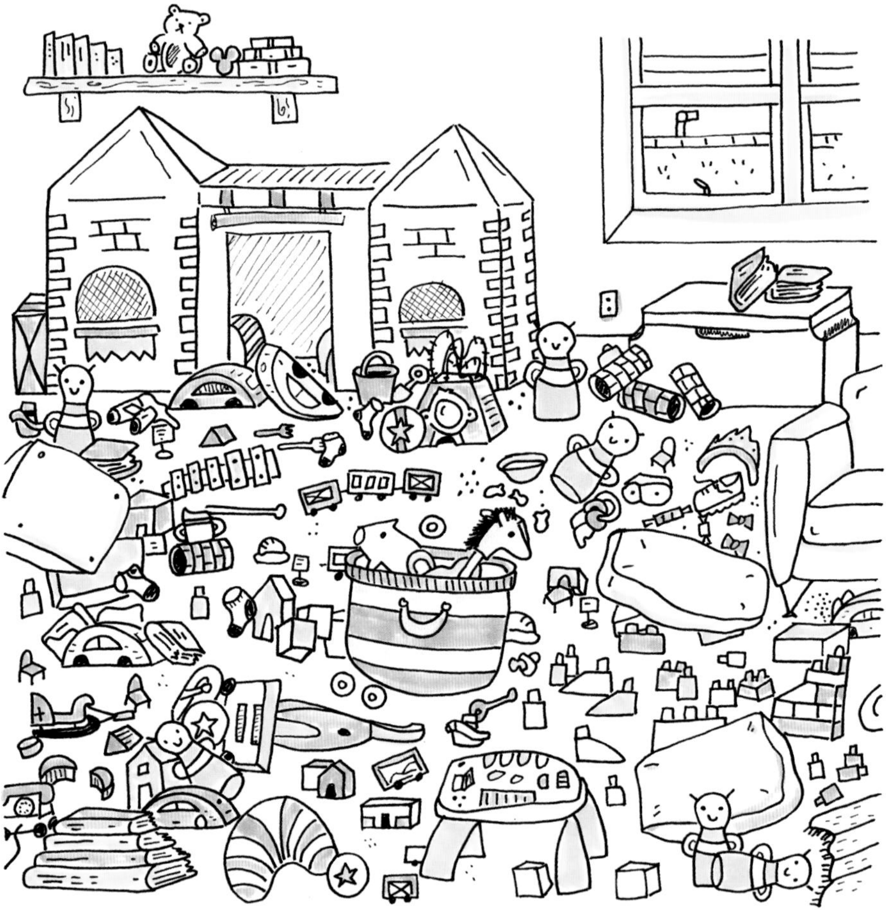

WHEN YOU'RE RUNNING LATE AND HAVE 10 SECONDS TO FIND THE SIPPY CUP....

RESPONSIBILITIES

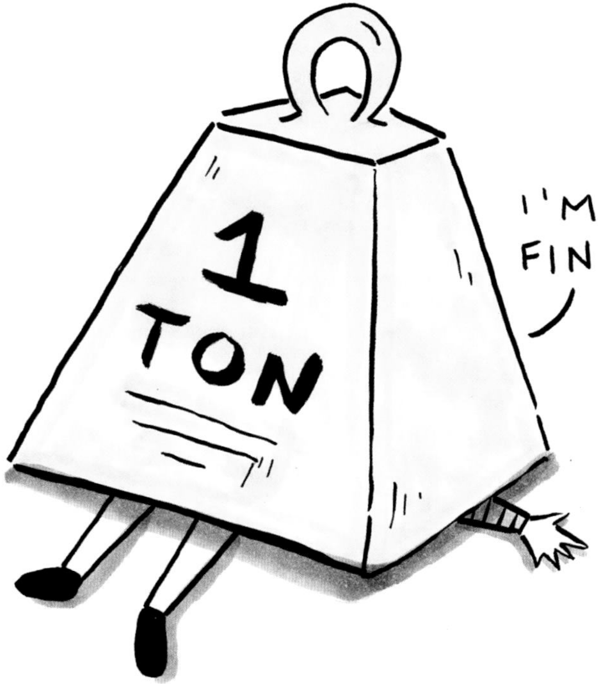
1
TON
I'M FINE

TARDY

NAME: **MOM**

DATE: **EVERY DAY**

TIME IN:

REASON: JUST ONE OF THOSE DAYS THAT THE KIDS WERE ACTING EXACTLY THE SAME AS ALWAYS.

☐ EXCUSED ☑ UNEXCUSED

MORE TARDIES

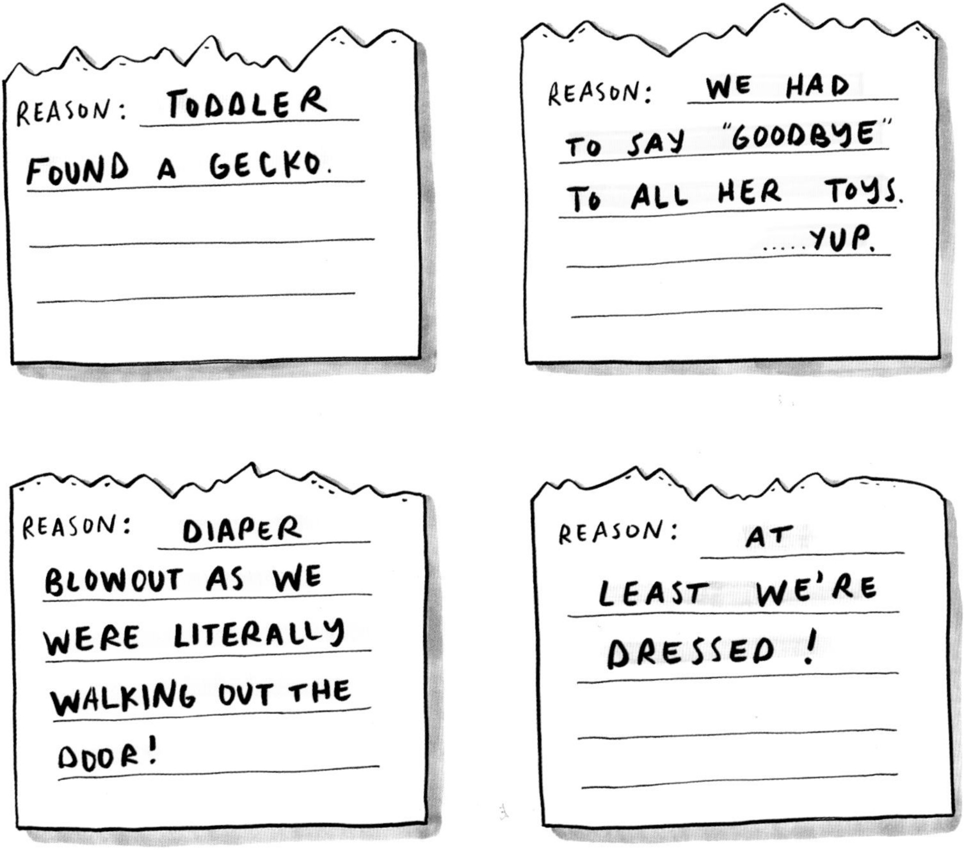
REASON: TODDLER FOUND A GECKO.
REASON: WE HAD TO SAY "GOODBYE" TO ALL HER TOYS. .....YUP.
REASON: DIAPER BLOWOUT AS WE WERE LITERALLY WALKING OUT THE DOOR!
REASON: AT LEAST WE'RE DRESSED!

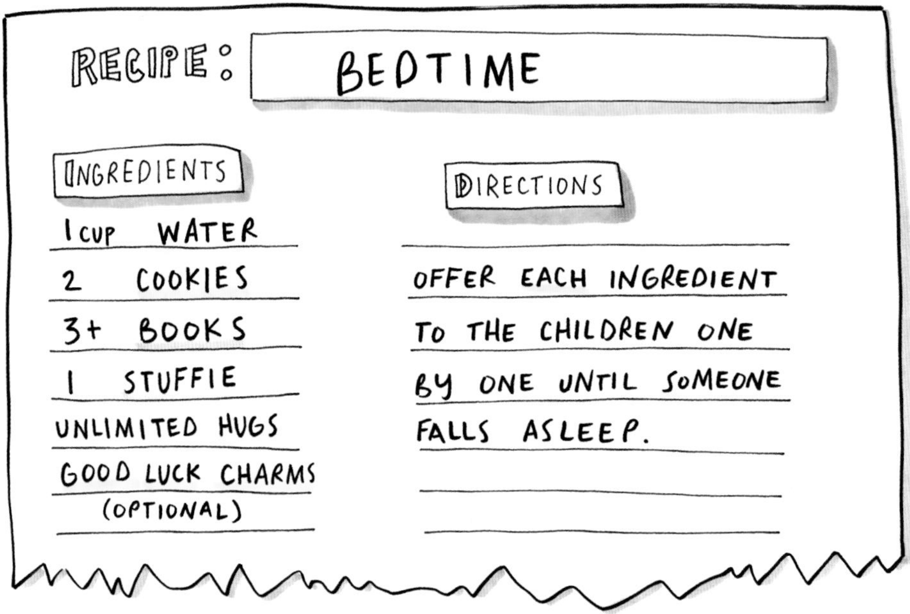
RECIPE: BEDTIME
INGREDIENTS
1 CUP WATER
2 COOKIES
3+ BOOKS
1 STUFFIE
UNLIMITED HUGS
GOOD LUCK CHARMS (OPTIONAL)
DIRECTIONS
OFFER EACH INGREDIENT TO THE CHILDREN ONE BY ONE UNTIL SOMEONE FALLS ASLEEP.

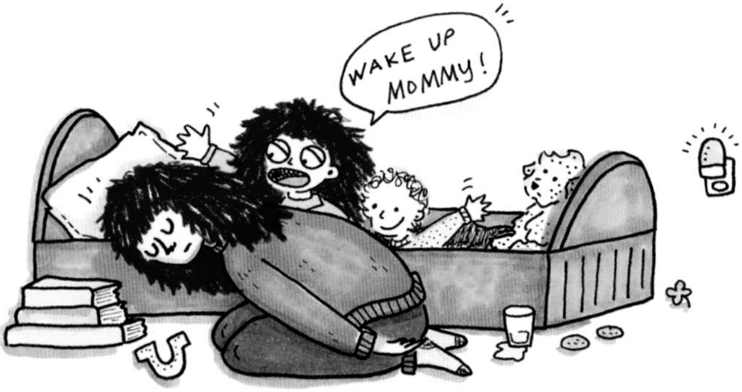
WAKE UP MOMMY!

DADDY'S STORY

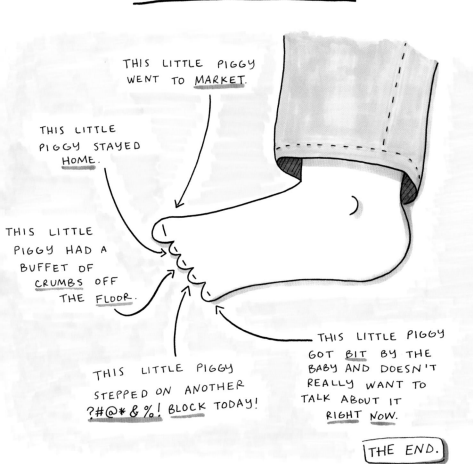

THIS LITTLE PIGGY WENT TO MARKET.

THIS LITTLE PIGGY STAYED HOME.

THIS LITTLE PIGGY HAD A BUFFET OF CRUMBS OFF THE FLOOR.

THIS LITTLE PIGGY STEPPED ON ANOTHER ?#@*&%! BLOCK TODAY!

THIS LITTLE PIGGY GOT BIT BY THE BABY AND DOESN'T REALLY WANT TO TALK ABOUT IT RIGHT NOW.

THE END.

MOTHERHOOD IS LIKE LAUNDRY.... IT NEVER ENDS.

(AND SOMETIMES IT'S SMELLY.)

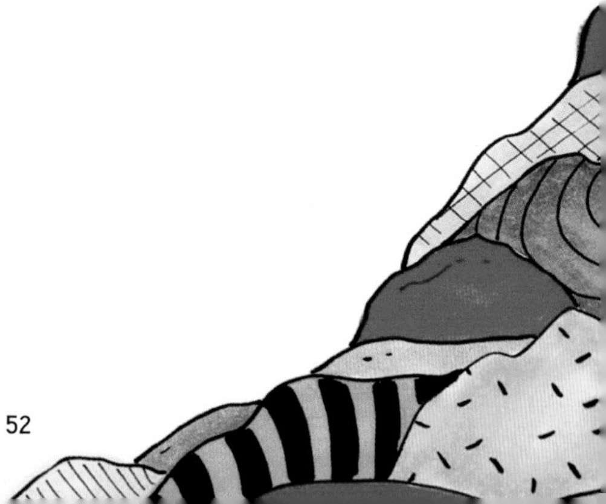

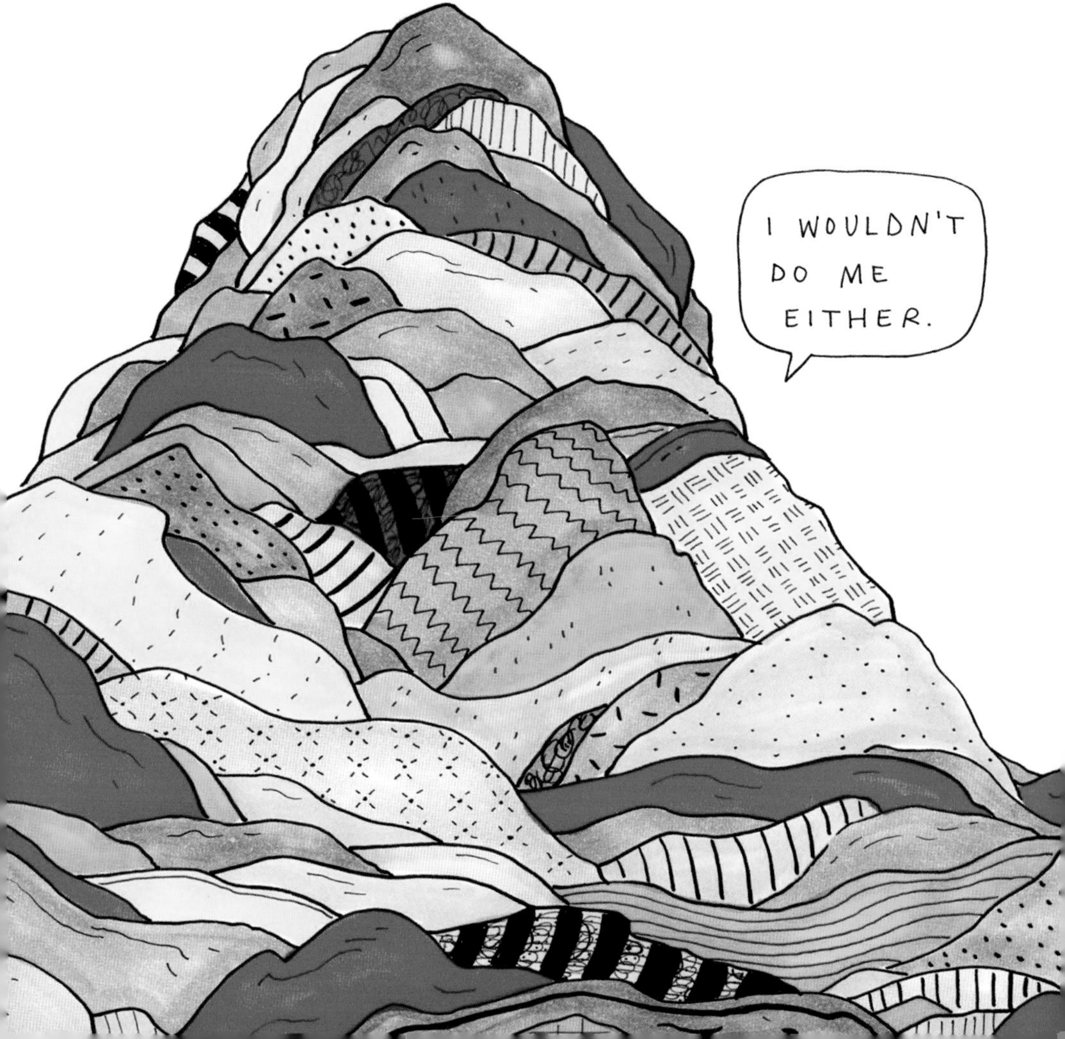
I WOULDN'T DO ME EITHER.

WHEN I
FEEL LIKE
I'M
HANGING
BY A
THREAD,

IT'S MY
FAMILY
THAT BRINGS
ME
BACK

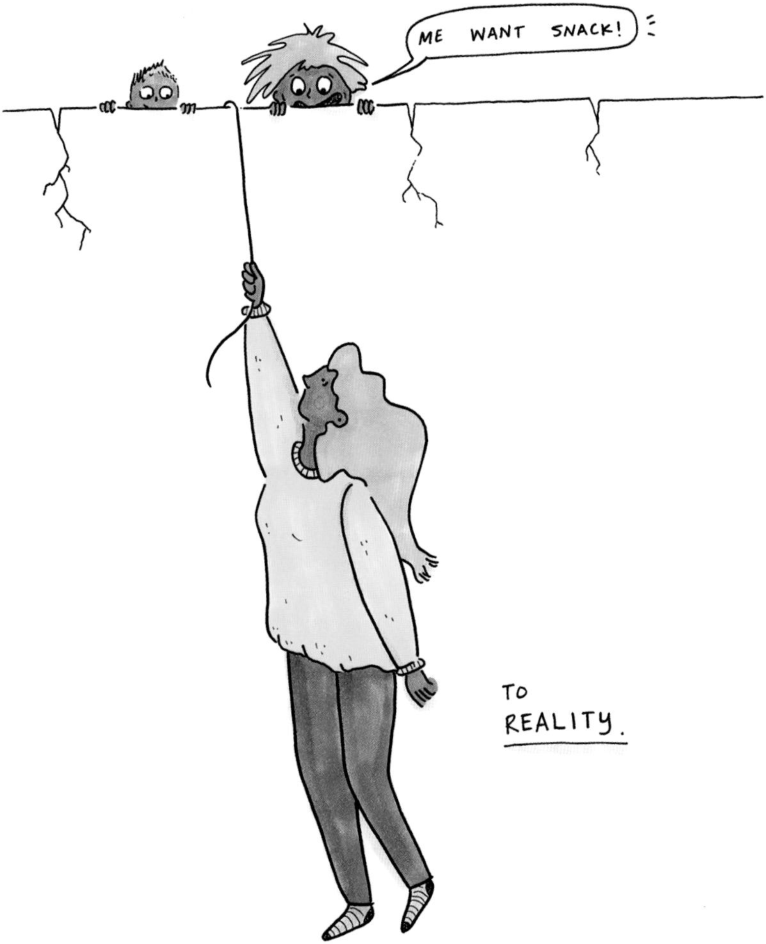
ME WANT SNACK!
TO
REALITY.

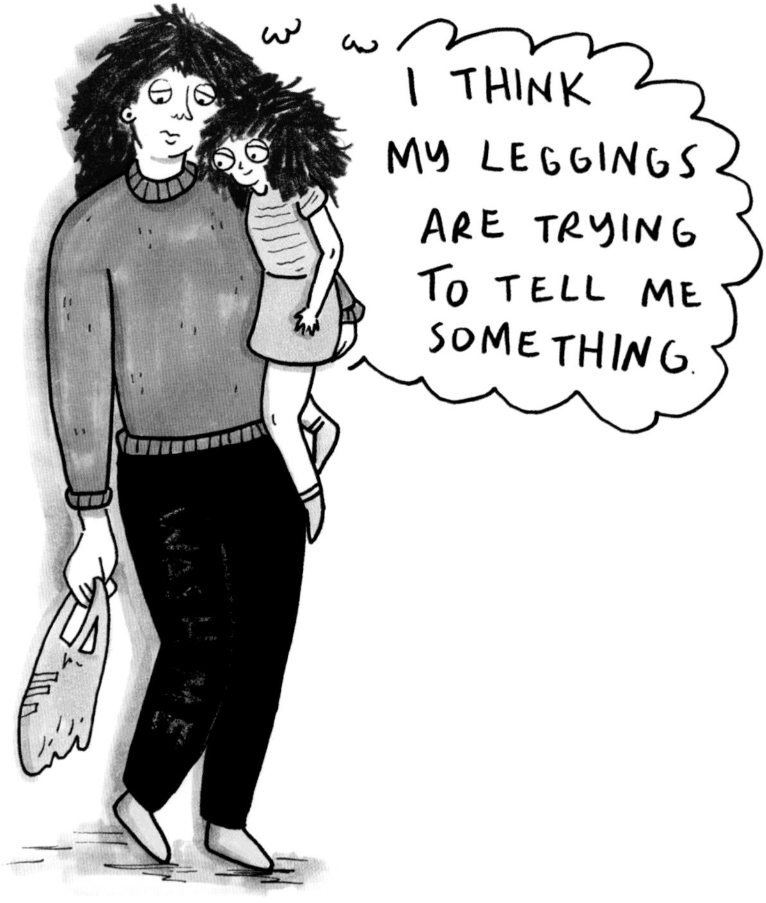
I THINK MY LEGGINGS ARE TRYING TO TELL ME SOMETHING.

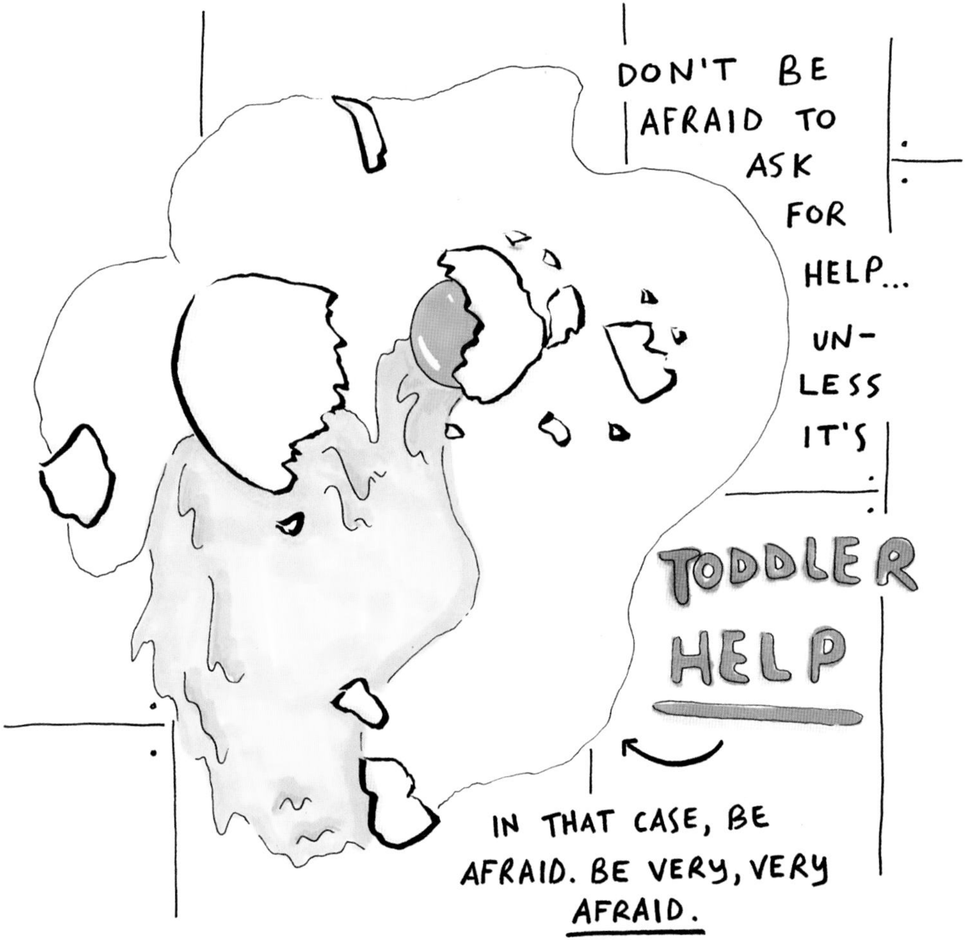
DON'T BE AFRAID TO ASK FOR HELP...
UN-LESS IT'S
TODDLER HELP
IN THAT CASE, BE AFRAID. BE VERY, VERY AFRAID.

BABY TALK

A VISUAL GUIDE FOR CURIOUS AUNTIES AND GRANDPARENTS

"PWILLOW"

"CAMEL-LOPE"

"MUGK"

"WAH-YA"

"TURNINING"

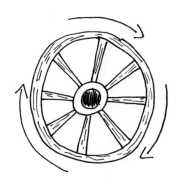

"PUG PUG"

WHAT DID I JUST SAY?

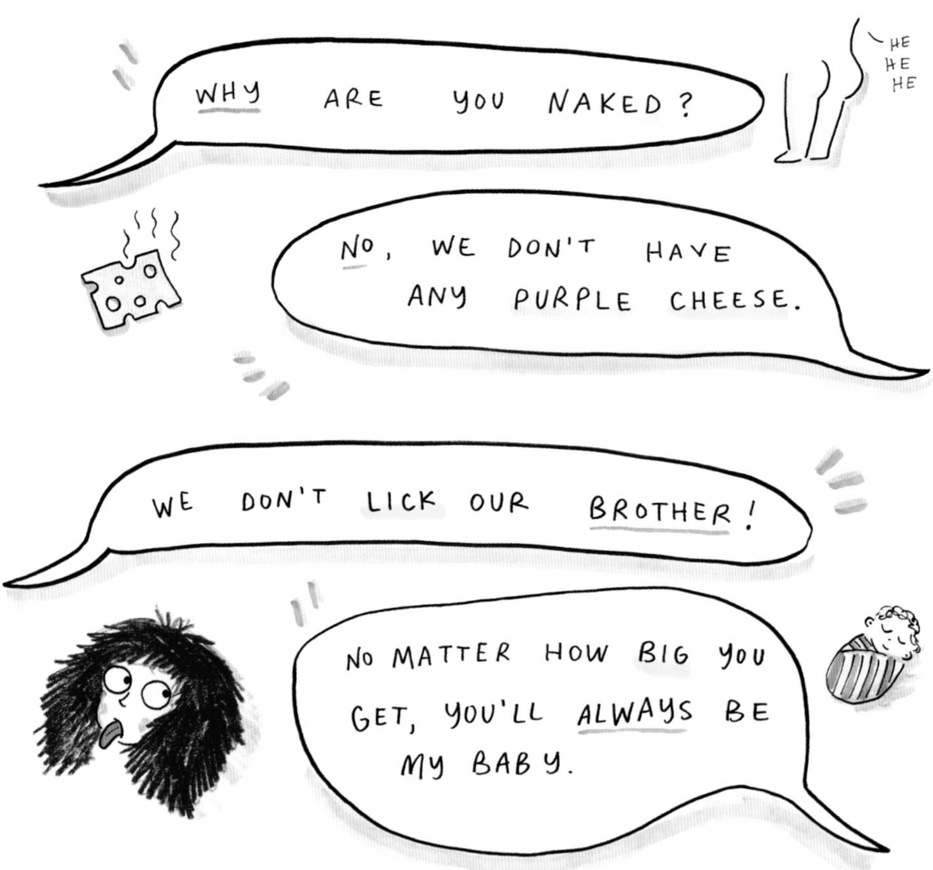
WHY ARE YOU NAKED?
HE HE HE
NO, WE DON'T HAVE ANY PURPLE CHEESE.
WE DON'T LICK OUR BROTHER!
NO MATTER HOW BIG YOU GET, YOU'LL ALWAYS BE MY BABY.

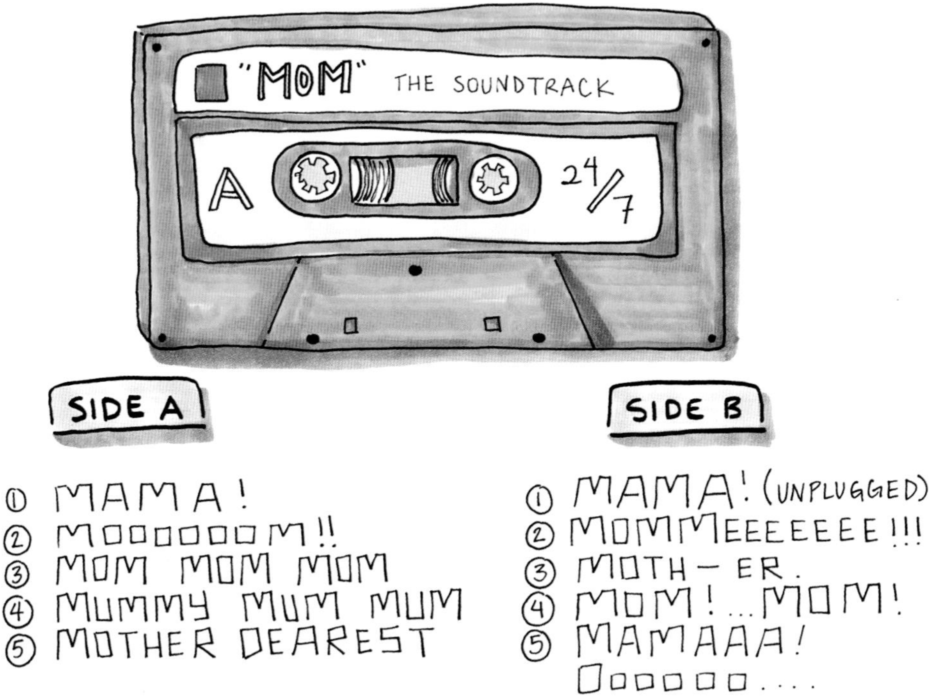
"MOM" THE SOUNDTRACK
A
24/7
SIDE A
① MAMA!
② MOOOOOOOM!!
③ MOM MOM MOM
④ MUMMY MUM MUM
⑤ MOTHER DEAREST
SIDE B
① MAMA! (UNPLUGGED)
② MOMMEEEEEEEE!!!
③ MOTH-ER.
④ MOM!...MOM!
⑤ MAMAAA!
OOOOOO....

LILY'S

FAVORITE:

FACE
TIME
CHATS

MATILDA & CLEO

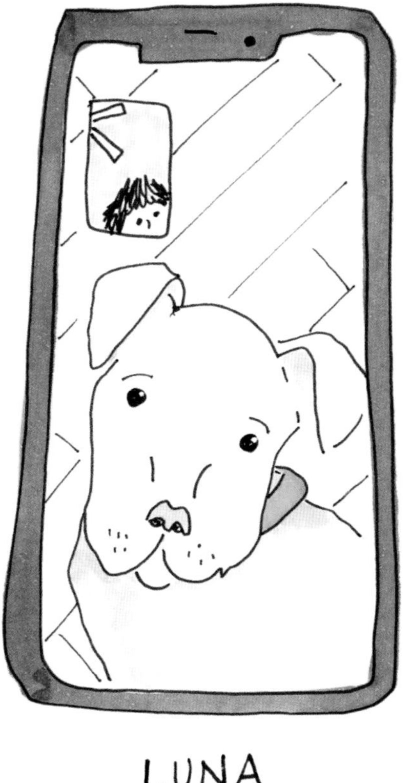

LUNA

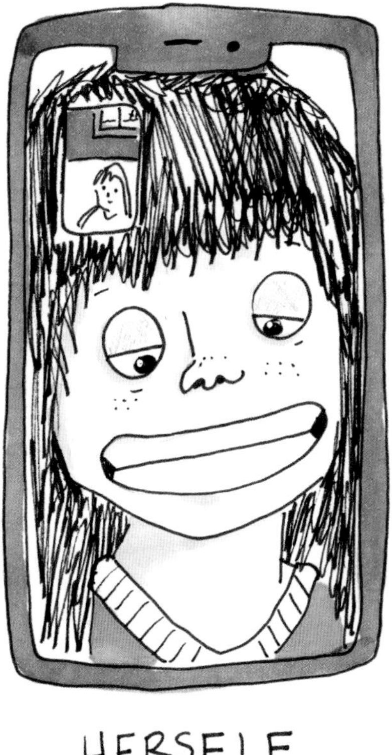

HERSELF

LOUD DADDY

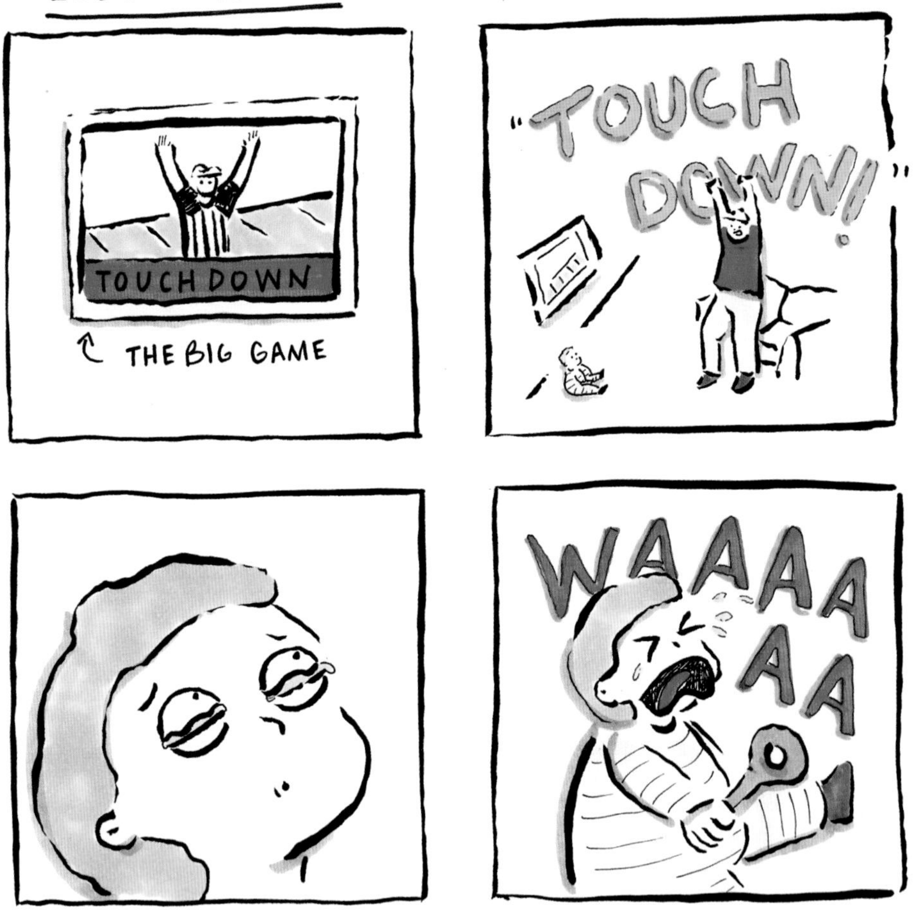
TOUCH DOWN
THE BIG GAME
"TOUCH DOWN!"
WAAAAAAA

BABY CARRIER SCIENCE

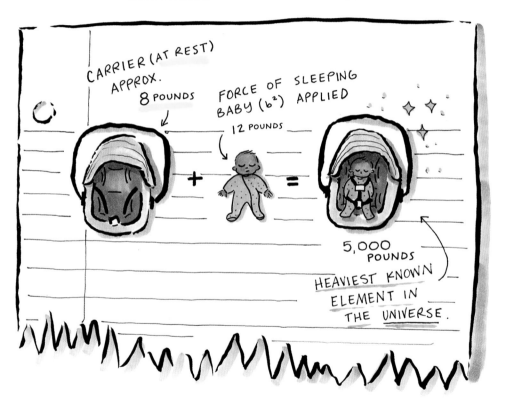

CARRIER (AT REST) APPROX. 8 POUNDS

FORCE OF SLEEPING BABY (b^2) APPLIED 12 POUNDS

+ =

5,000 POUNDS

HEAVIEST KNOWN ELEMENT IN THE UNIVERSE.

IT'S A GIRL

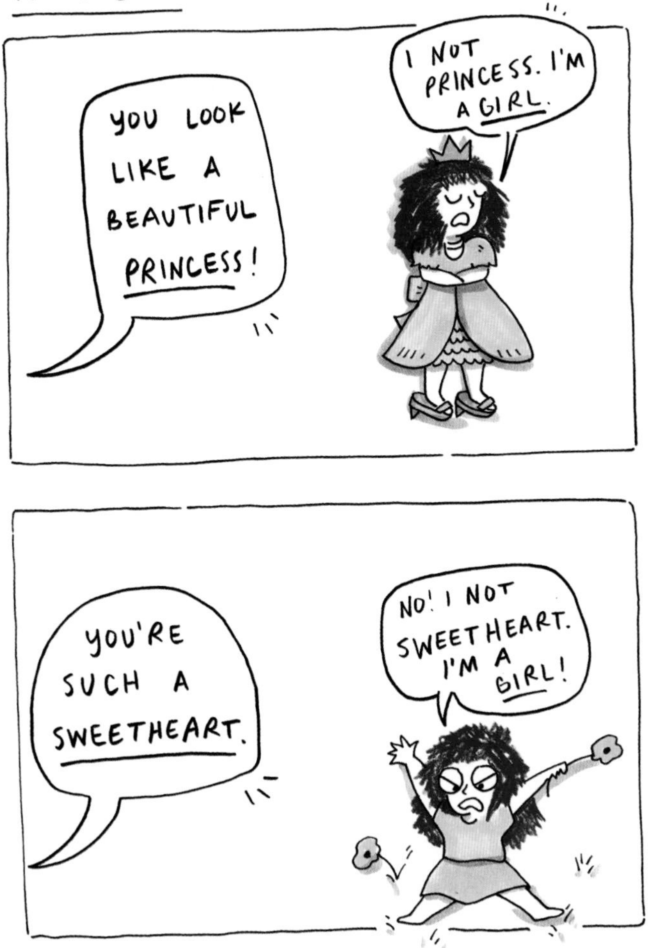
YOU LOOK LIKE A BEAUTIFUL PRINCESS!
I NOT PRINCESS. I'M A GIRL.
YOU'RE SUCH A SWEETHEART.
NO! I NOT SWEETHEART. I'M A GIRL!

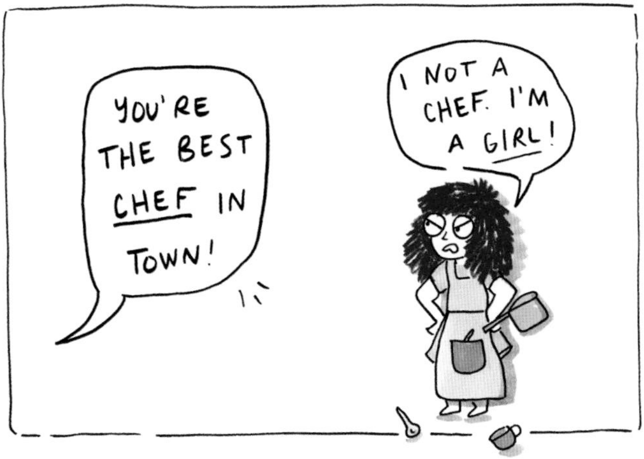
YOU'RE THE BEST CHEF IN TOWN!
I NOT A CHEF. I'M A GIRL!

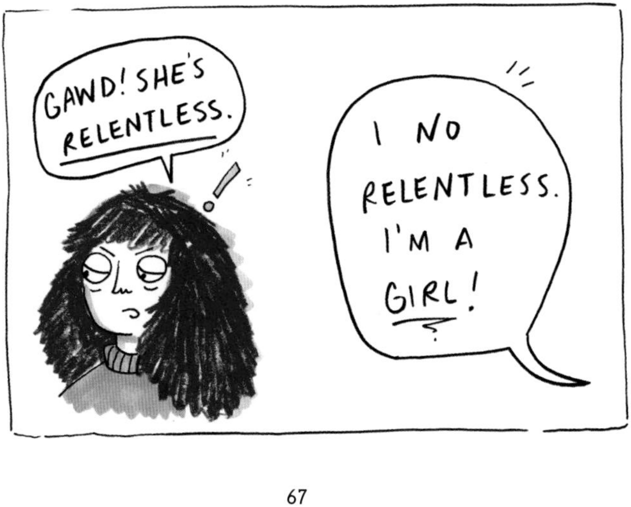
GAWD! SHE'S RELENTLESS.
I NO RELENTLESS. I'M A GIRL!

CURRENTLY LIVING UNDER A PILE OF

LAUNDRY

DISHES

TOYS

HUGS

DIAPERS

REASONS MY 3-YEAR-OLD RAN TO HER ROOM AND CRIED.

I PEELED HER ORANGE WRONG.

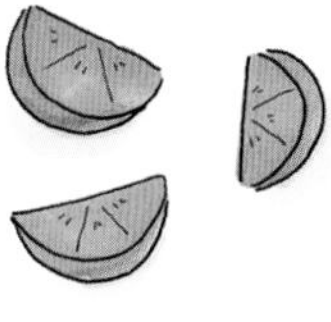

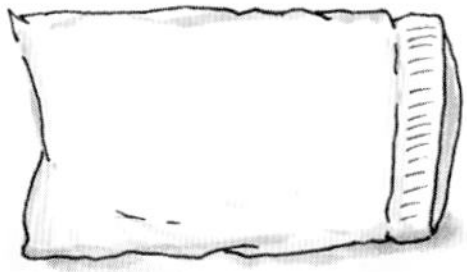

DADDY SLEPT IN TOO LATE.

HER PRINCESS CUP WAS IN THE DISHWASHER.

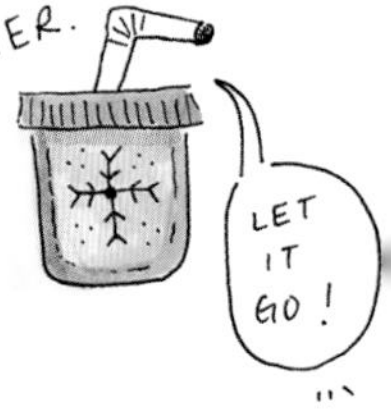
LET IT GO!

THE FLY

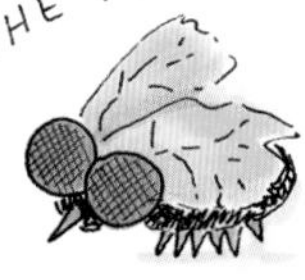

WOULDN'T SHOO.

GRANDPA DOESN'T HAVE A CAT.

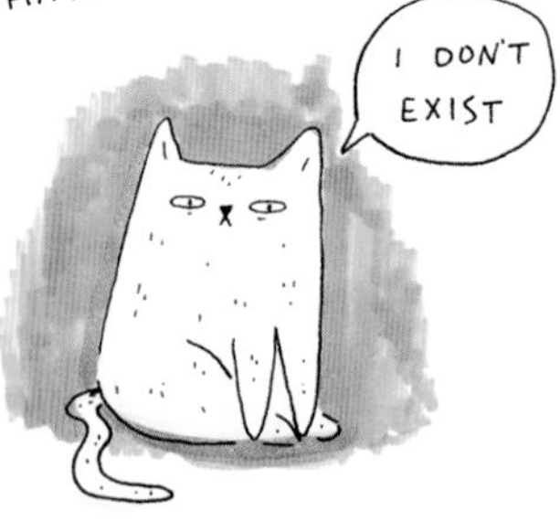
I DON'T EXIST

HER ICE CREAM WAS COLD.

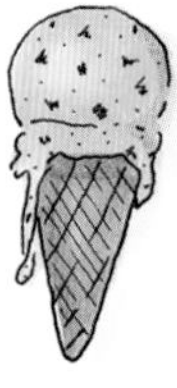

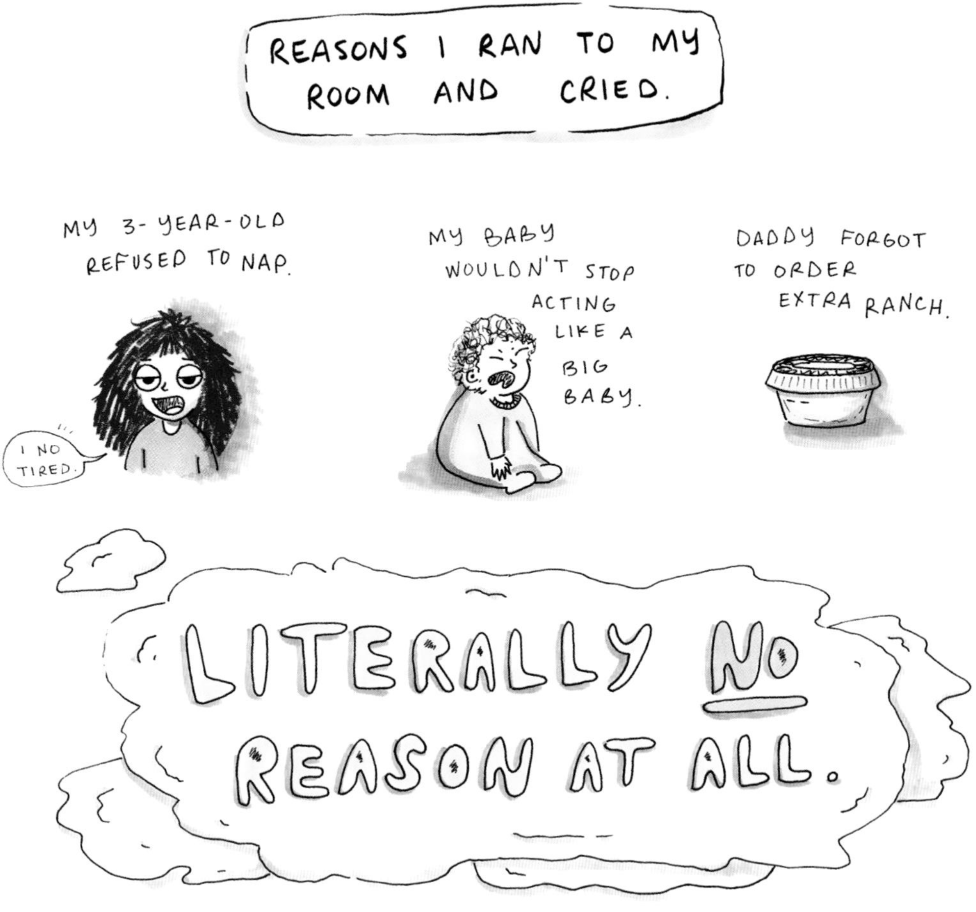
REASONS I RAN TO MY ROOM AND CRIED.
MY 3-YEAR-OLD REFUSED TO NAP.
I NO TIRED.
MY BABY WOULDN'T STOP ACTING LIKE A BIG BABY.
DADDY FORGOT TO ORDER EXTRA RANCH.
LITERALLY NO REASON AT ALL.

WE ALL CRIED TODAY

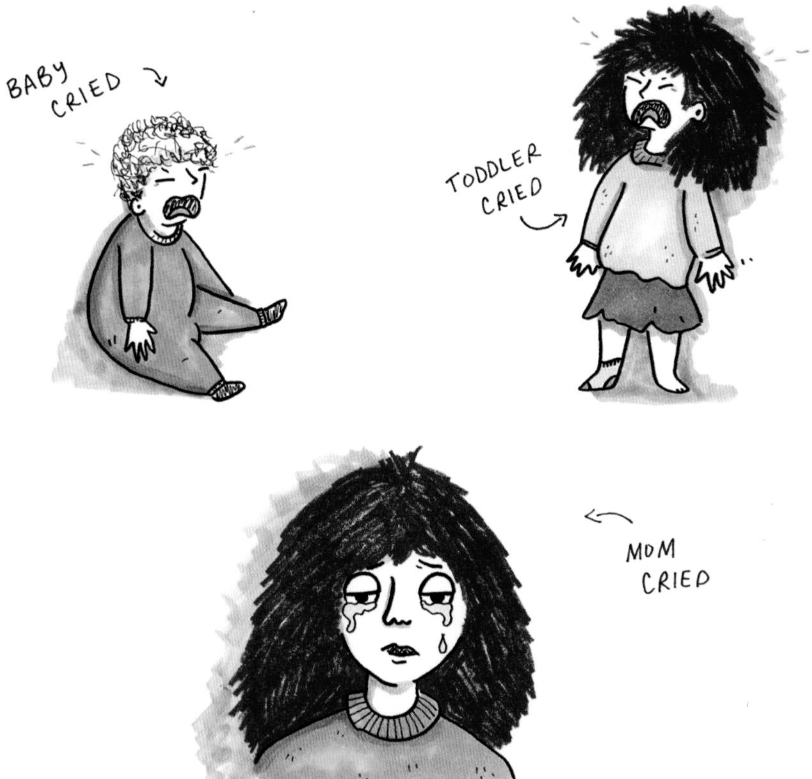
BABY CRIED
TODDLER CRIED
MOM CRIED

AND THEN THE POST-CRY NAP

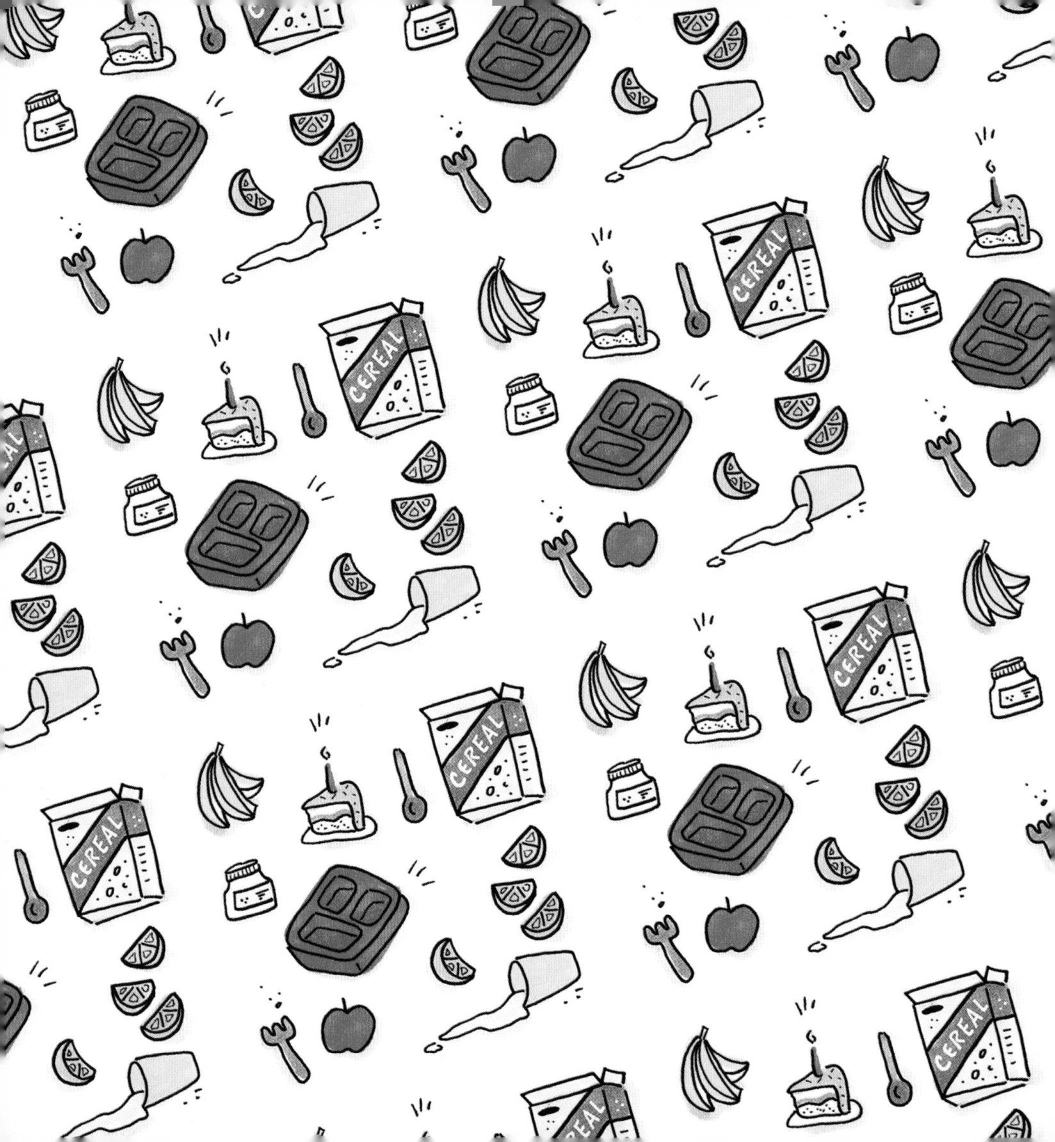
CEREAL

③

FOOD WARS

THESE ARE NOT THE SNACKS YOU ARE LOOKING FOR . . .

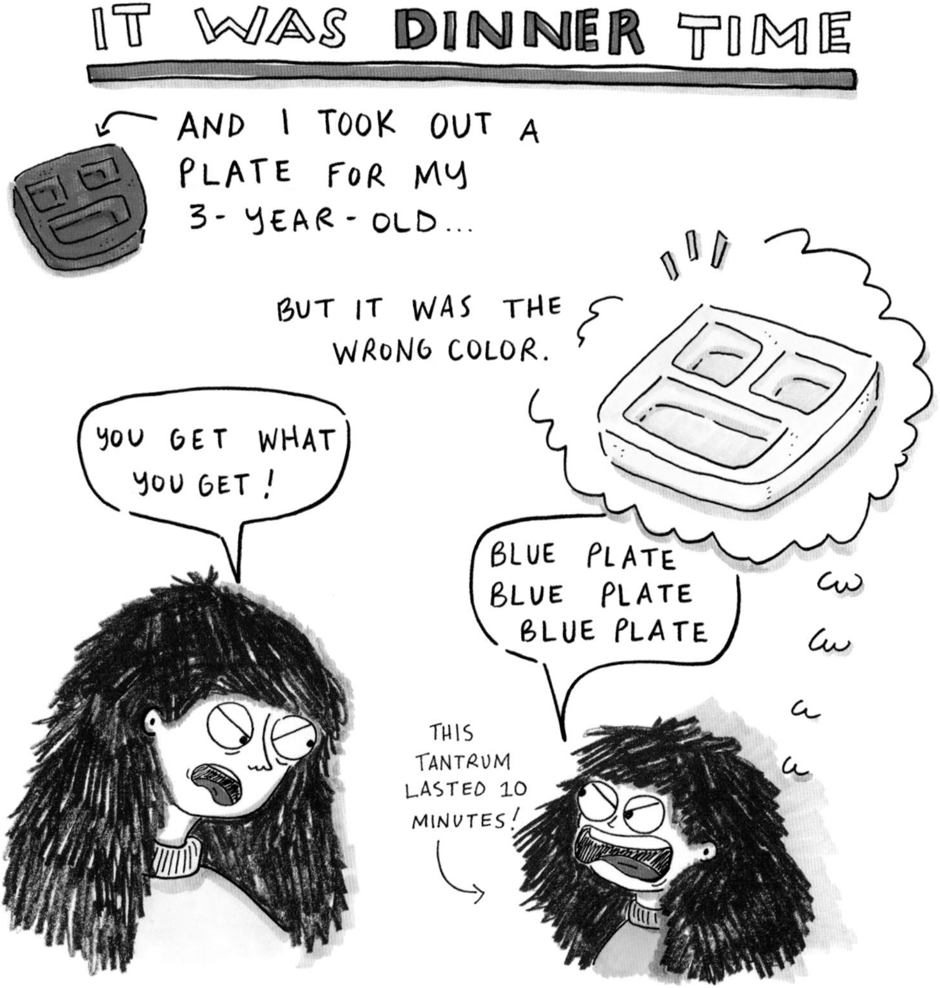
IT WAS DINNER TIME
AND I TOOK OUT A PLATE FOR MY 3-YEAR-OLD...
BUT IT WAS THE WRONG COLOR.
YOU GET WHAT YOU GET!
BLUE PLATE BLUE PLATE BLUE PLATE
THIS TANTRUM LASTED 10 MINUTES!

SO, WE HAD
ICE CREAM
FOR DINNER.

ON THE
<u>RED</u> PLATE.

I WIN.

TODDLER HAPPY HOUR

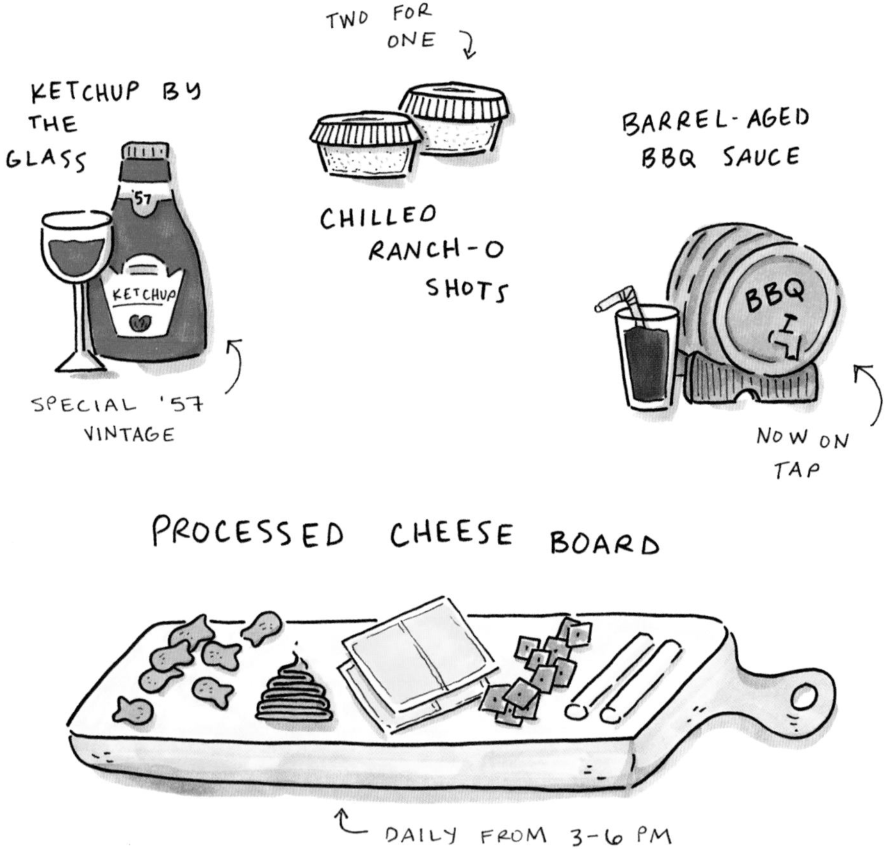
TWO FOR ONE
KETCHUP BY THE GLASS
'57
KETCHUP
CHILLED RANCH-O SHOTS
BARREL-AGED BBQ SAUCE
BBQ
SPECIAL '57 VINTAGE
NOW ON TAP
PROCESSED CHEESE BOARD
DAILY FROM 3-6 PM

I ATE MY KID'S COOKIE AT NAP TIME.

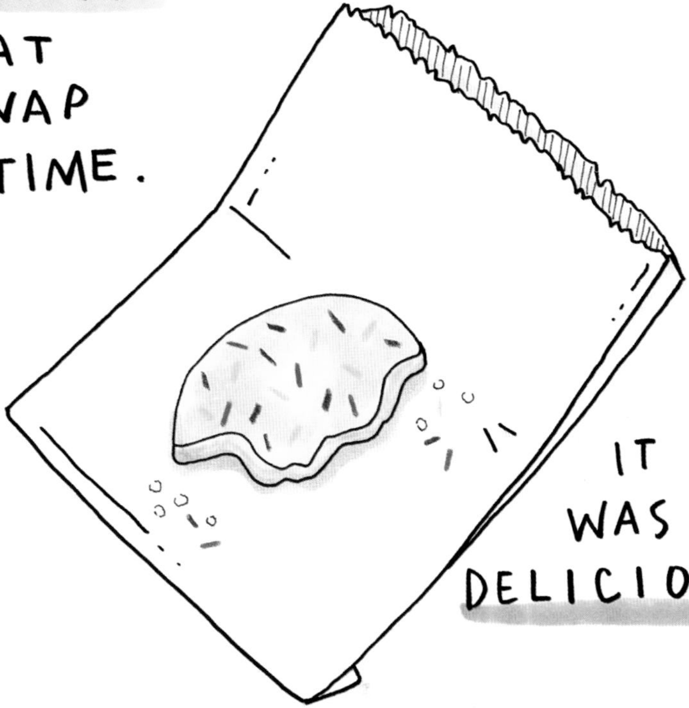

IT WAS DELICIOUS.

IF THE THINGS MY BABY

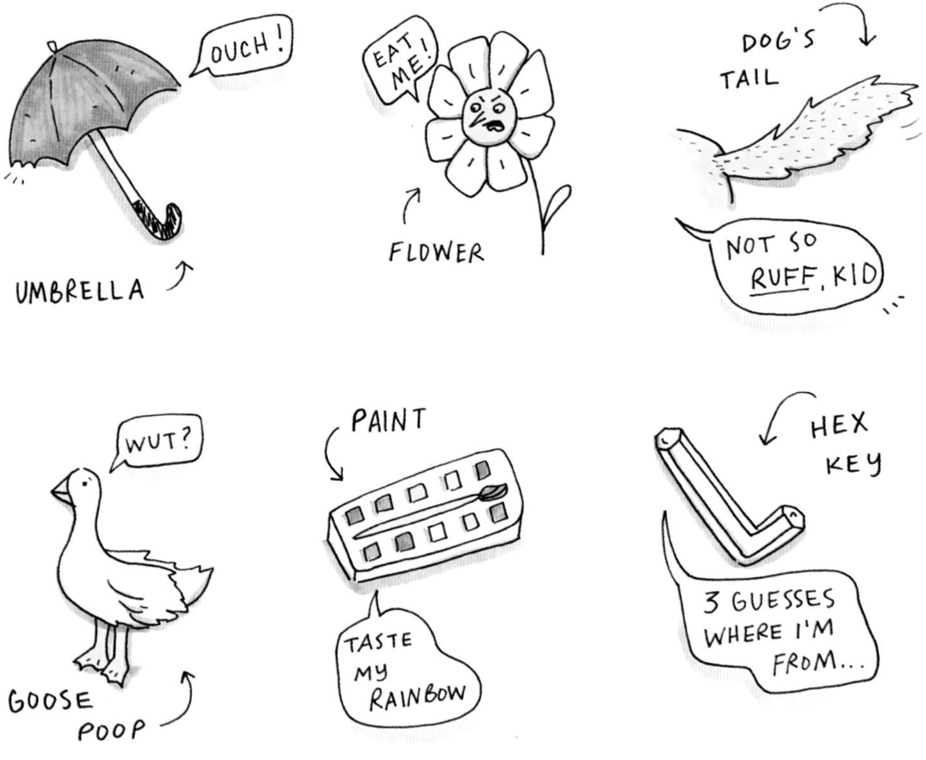
OUCH!
UMBRELLA
EAT ME!
FLOWER
DOG'S TAIL
NOT SO RUFF, KID
WUT?
GOOSE POOP
PAINT
TASTE MY RAINBOW
HEX KEY
3 GUESSES WHERE I'M FROM...

TRIED TO EAT COULD TALK

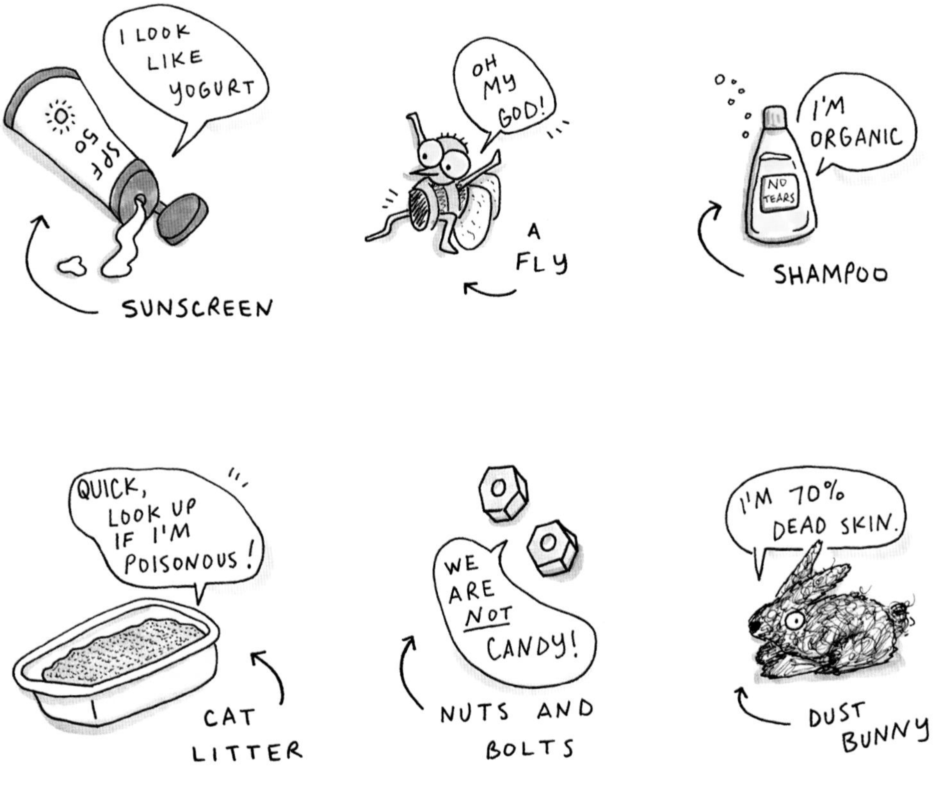
I LOOK LIKE YOGURT
SPF 50
SUNSCREEN
OH MY GOD!
A FLY
I'M ORGANIC
NO TEARS
SHAMPOO
QUICK, LOOK UP IF I'M POISONOUS!
CAT LITTER
WE ARE NOT CANDY!
NUTS AND BOLTS
I'M 70% DEAD SKIN.
DUST BUNNY

WHAT'S FOR DINNER?

DEFINITELY
NOT GOING TO
EAT THESE LEFTOVERS

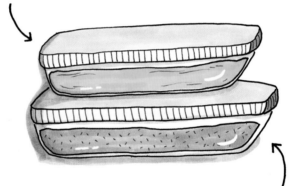

BETTER LET THEM
ROT IN THE BACK OF
MY FRIDGE FOR ANOTHER
TWO WEEKS ANYWAY.

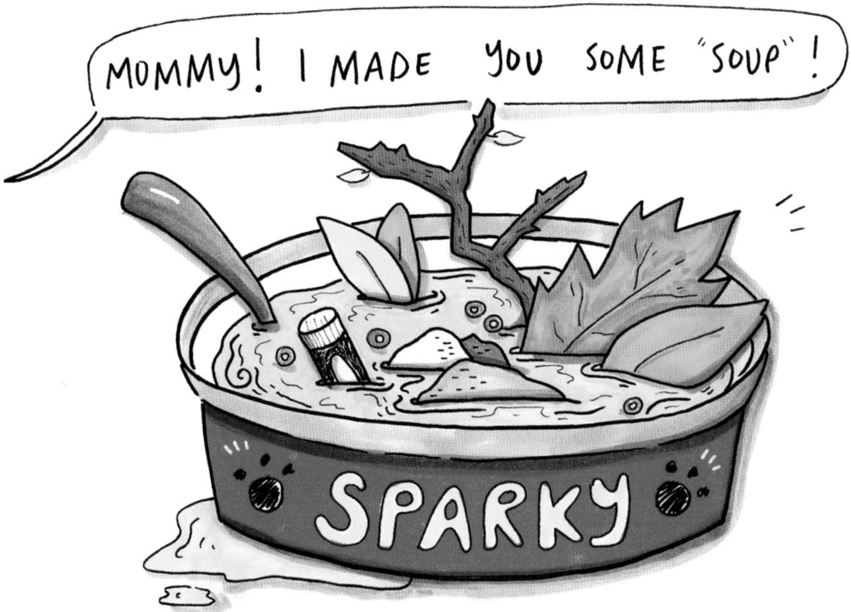
MOMMY! I MADE YOU SOME "SOUP"!
SPARKY

MY DEEPEST APOLOGIES

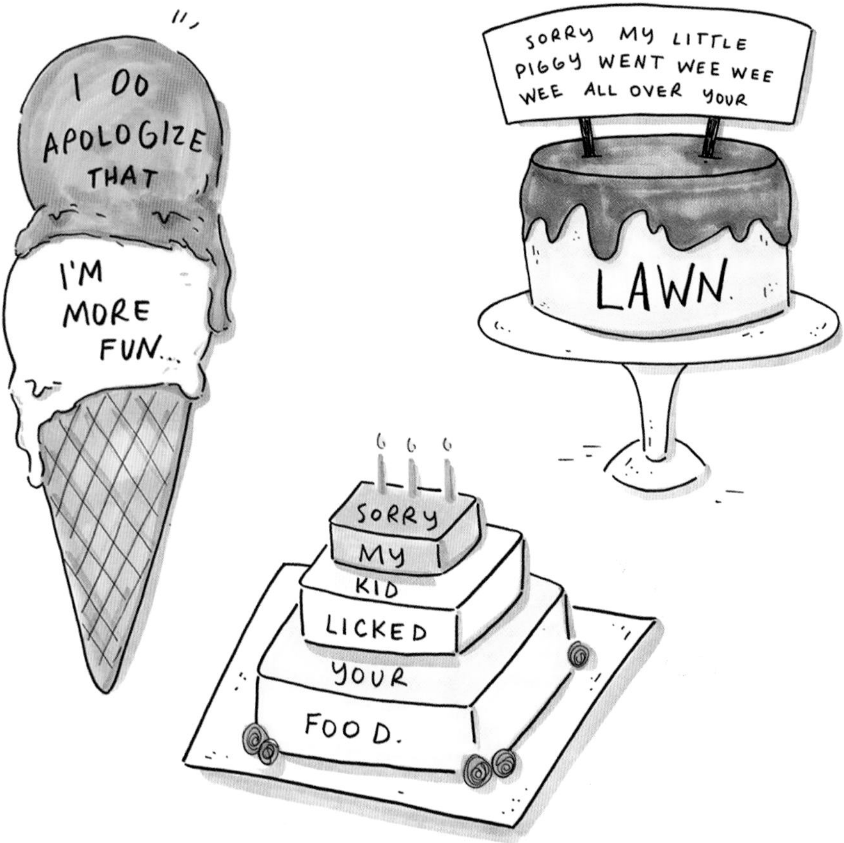
I DO APOLOGIZE THAT
I'M MORE FUN...
SORRY MY LITTLE PIGGY WENT WEE WEE WEE ALL OVER YOUR
LAWN.
SORRY MY KID LICKED YOUR FOOD.

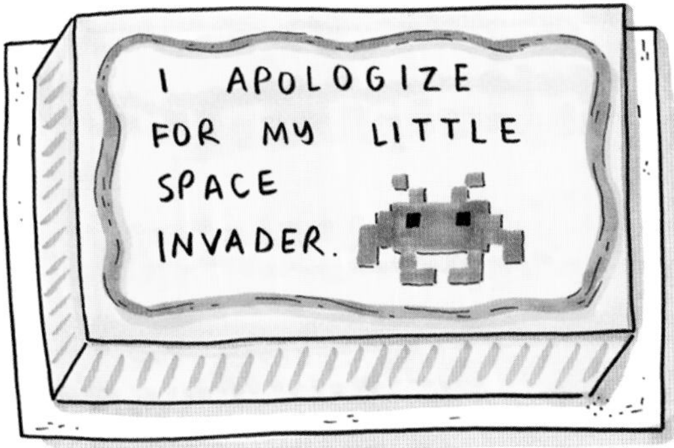
I APOLOGIZE FOR MY LITTLE SPACE INVADER.

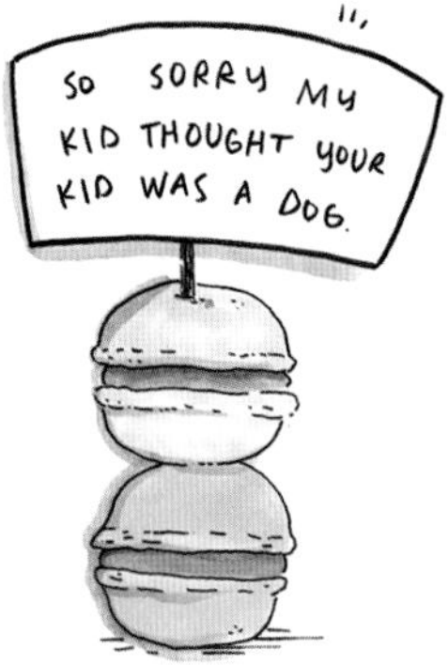
SO SORRY MY KID THOUGHT YOUR KID WAS A DOG.

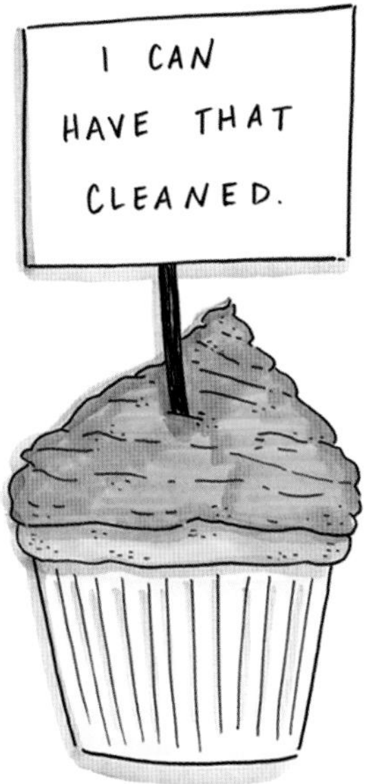
I CAN HAVE THAT CLEANED.

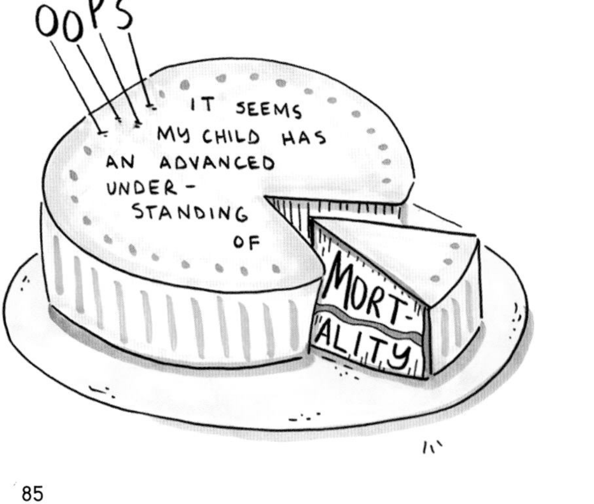
OOPS
IT SEEMS MY CHILD HAS AN ADVANCED UNDER-STANDING OF
MORT-ALITY

BABY BLENDER HACKS

5 NEW USES TO KEEP THAT TINY PIECE OF JUNK OUT OF THE LANDFILL.

DOOR STOP

PAPER SHREDDER

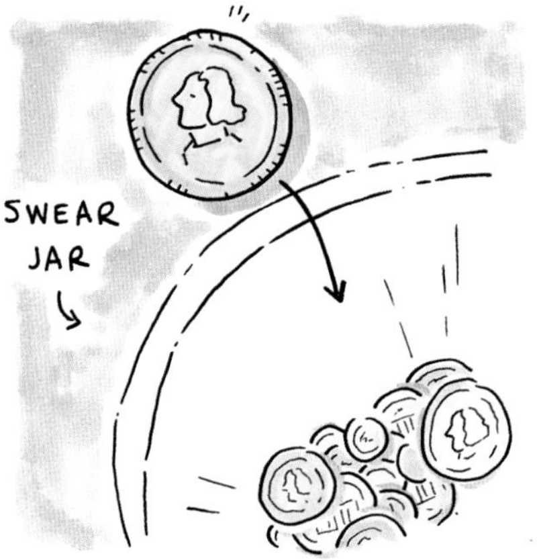
SWEAR
JAR

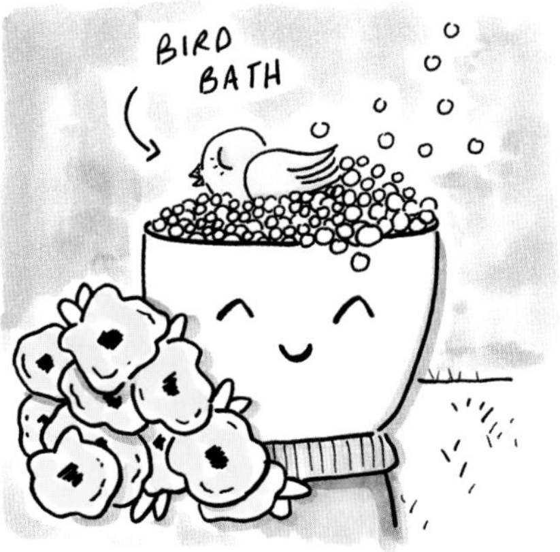
BIRD
BATH

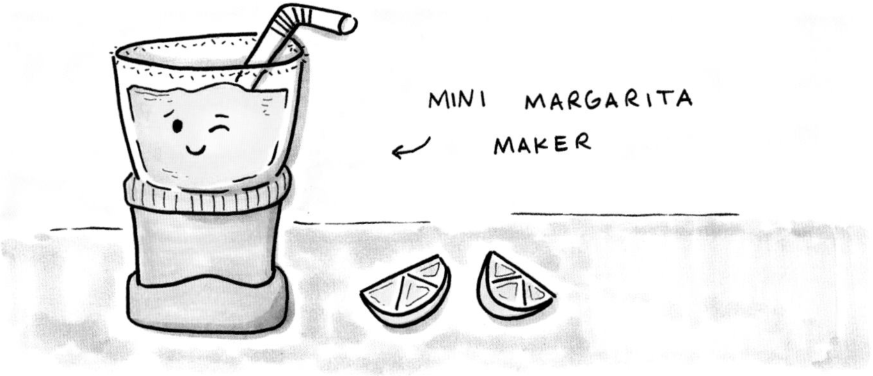
MINI MARGARITA
MAKER

BIBDANAS EXPLAINED

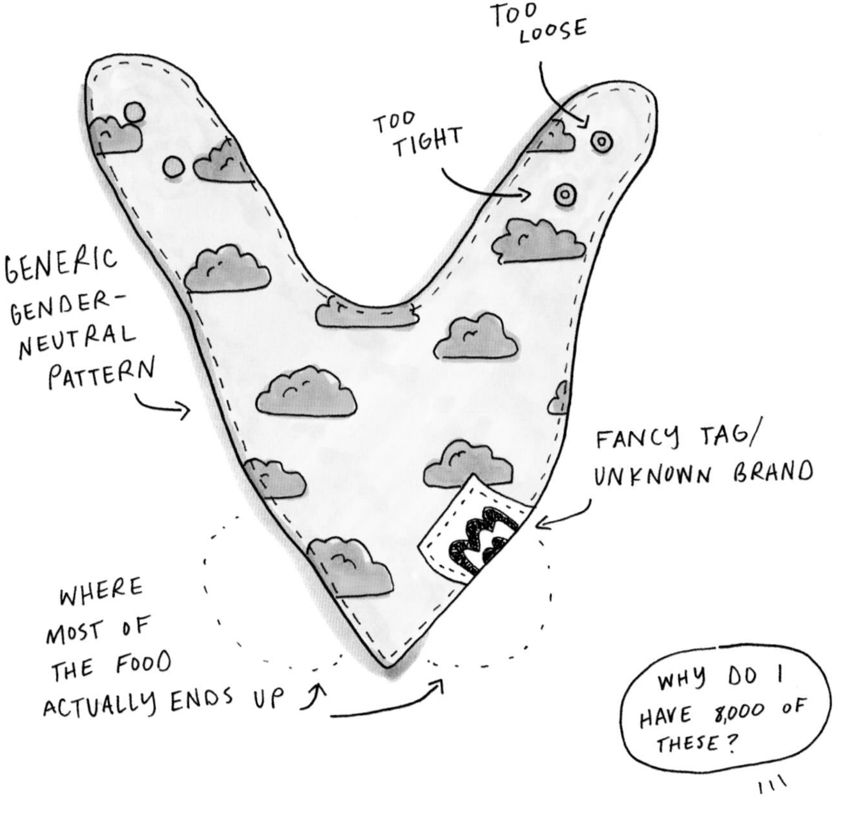
TOO LOOSE
TOO TIGHT
GENERIC GENDER-NEUTRAL PATTERN
FANCY TAG/ UNKNOWN BRAND
WHERE MOST OF THE FOOD ACTUALLY ENDS UP
WHY DO I HAVE 8,000 OF THESE?

BOWL COLOR CHART

FOR EASY REFERENCE

RED	OKAY FOR APPLES, STRAWBERRIES, AND WATERMELON
YELLOW	MAC AND CHEESE ONLY!
BLUE	THE "CEREAL" BOWL SOMETIMES BLUEBERRIES
ORANGE	PERFECT FOR PEACHES, ORANGES, AND OBVIOUSLY GOLDFISHIES
WHITE	AN ADEQUATE REPLACEMENT IF ORANGE, BLUE, OR RED ARE DIRTY (<u>NOT</u> YELLOW!)
GREEN	SHALL NEVER BE USED UNDER ANY CIRCUMSTANCE

BITE NEGOTIATIONS

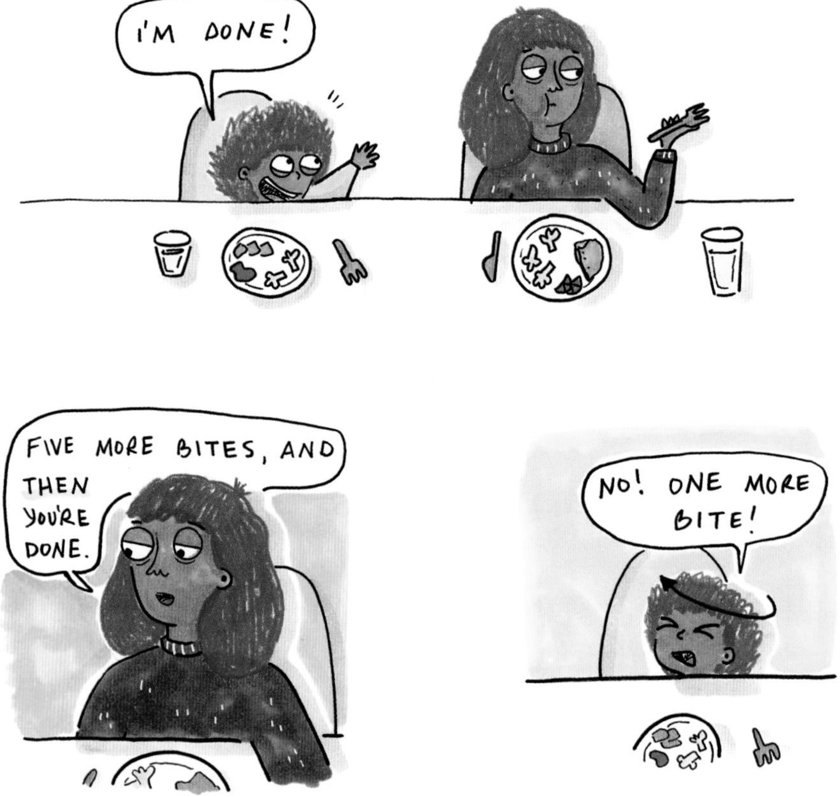
I'M DONE!
FIVE MORE BITES, AND THEN YOU'RE DONE.
NO! ONE MORE BITE!

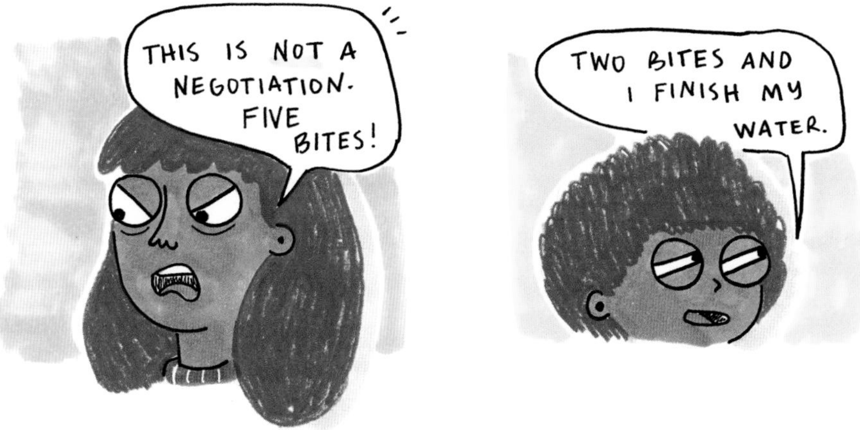
THIS IS NOT A NEGOTIATION. FIVE BITES!
TWO BITES AND I FINISH MY WATER.

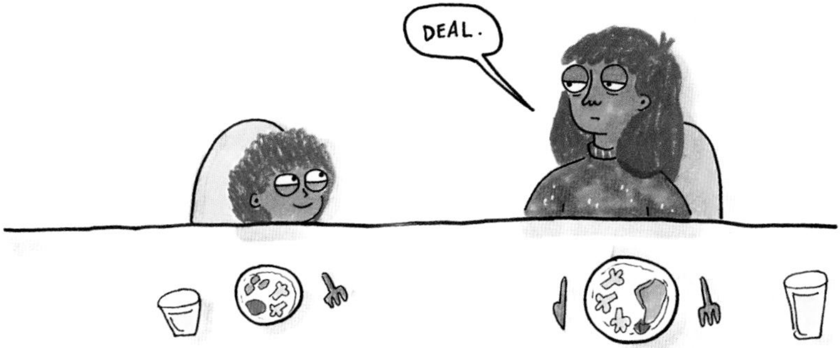
DEAL.

WONDER POUCH

WHO NEEDS TEETH WHEN YOUR KID CAN SURVIVE ON GOO FOR AT LEAST 6 YEARS!

"NUGGETS" ALWAYS TASTE BETTER

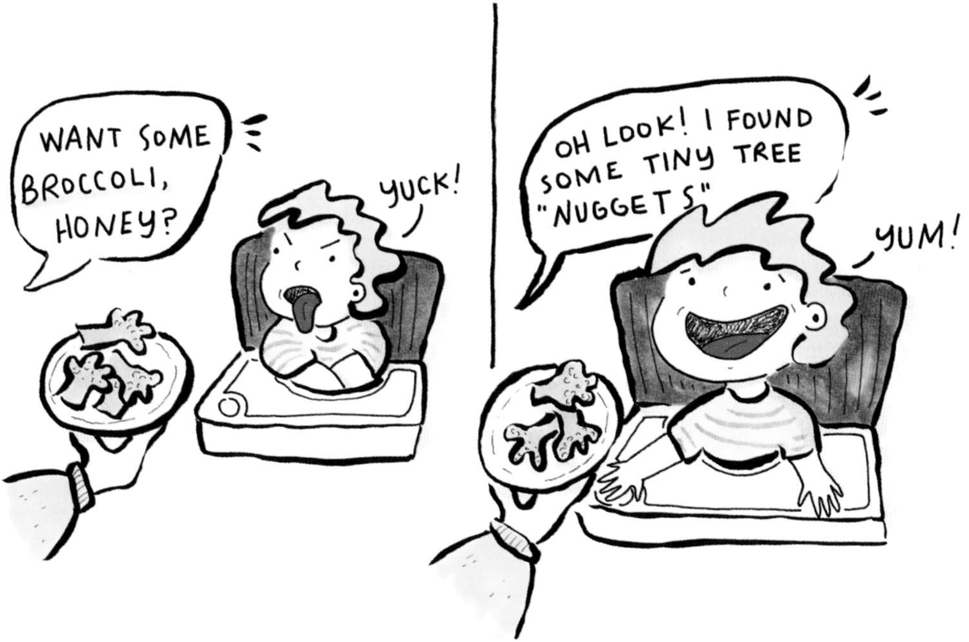
WANT SOME BROCCOLI, HONEY?
YUCK!
OH LOOK! I FOUND SOME TINY TREE "NUGGETS"
YUM!

ONE BANANA, TWO BANANA
THREE BANANA, <u>FOUR</u>!

WHEN MOMMY GETS
NEW BANANAS,
I SHALL EAT <u>NO</u> <u>MORE</u>!

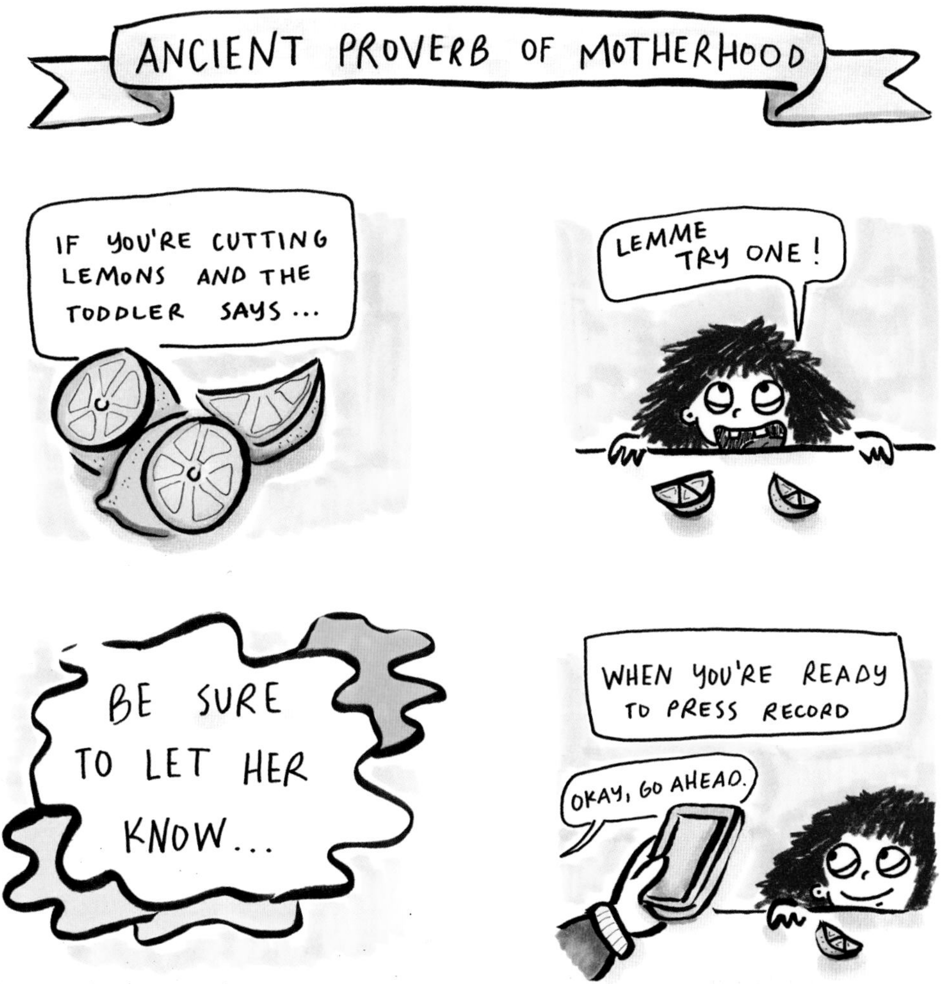
ANCIENT PROVERB OF MOTHERHOOD
IF YOU'RE CUTTING LEMONS AND THE TODDLER SAYS...
LEMME TRY ONE!
BE SURE TO LET HER KNOW...
WHEN YOU'RE READY TO PRESS RECORD
OKAY, GO AHEAD.

EMPTY TRAY, HIDDEN DINNER

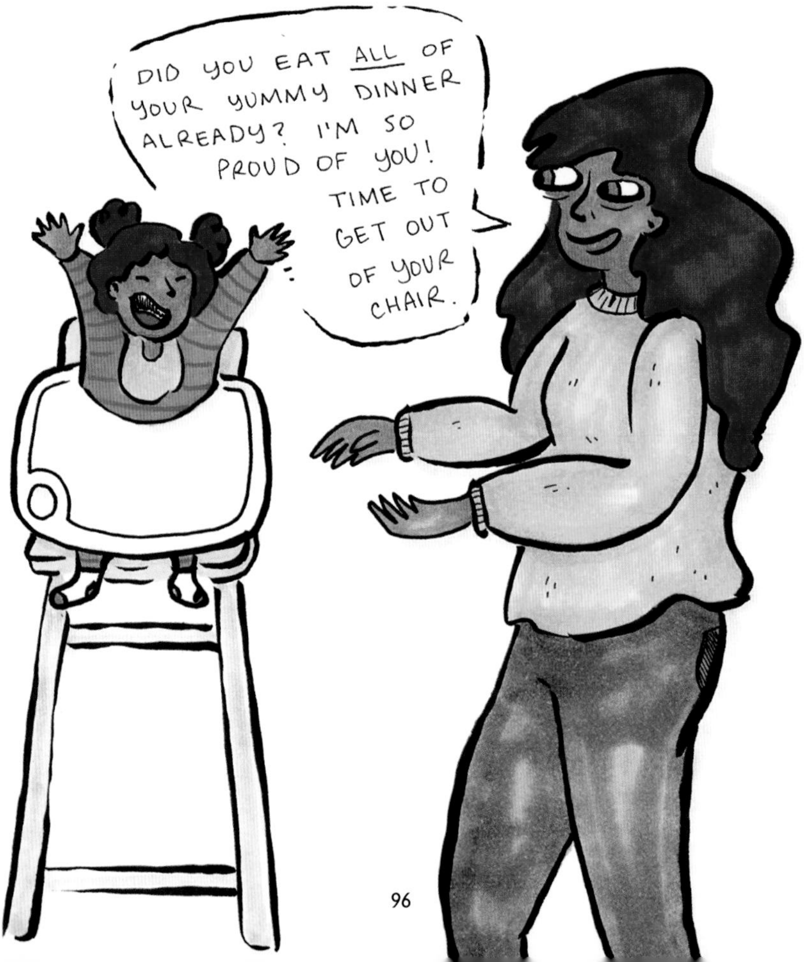
DID YOU EAT ALL OF YOUR YUMMY DINNER ALREADY? I'M SO PROUD OF YOU! TIME TO GET OUT OF YOUR CHAIR.

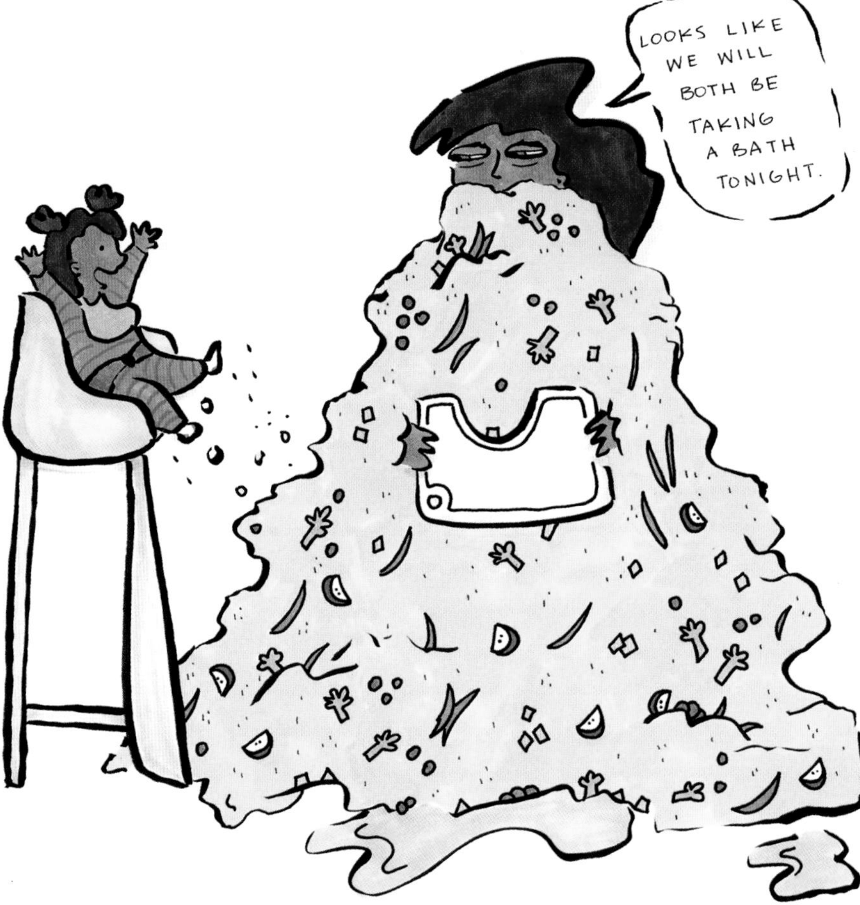
LOOKS LIKE WE WILL BOTH BE TAKING A BATH TONIGHT.

FOODS MY KID LOVED LAST WEEK BUT HATES NOW

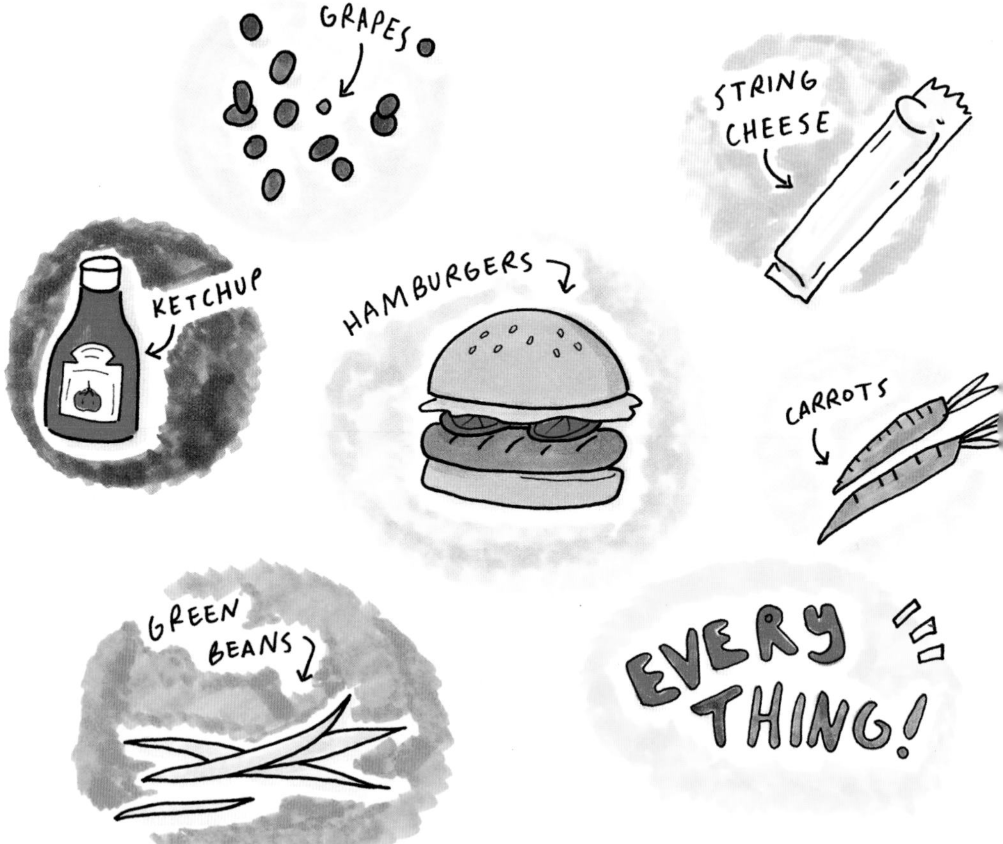
GRAPES
STRING CHEESE
KETCHUP
HAMBURGERS
CARROTS
GREEN BEANS
EVERY THING!

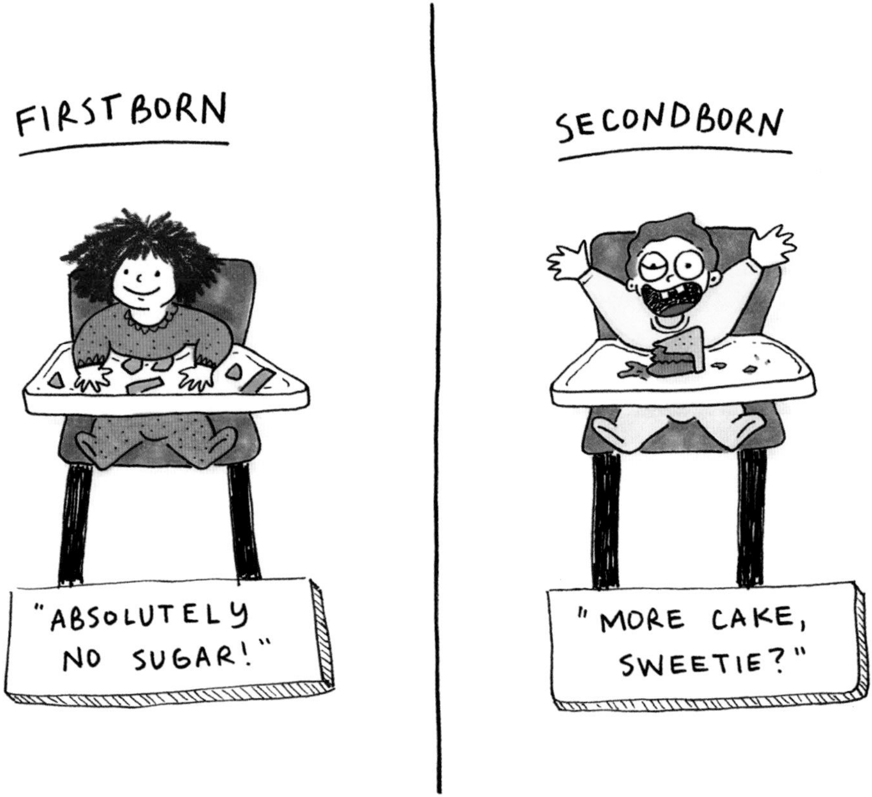
FIRSTBORN
SECONDBORN
"ABSOLUTELY NO SUGAR!"
"MORE CAKE, SWEETIE?"

MY BABY, THE VACUUM

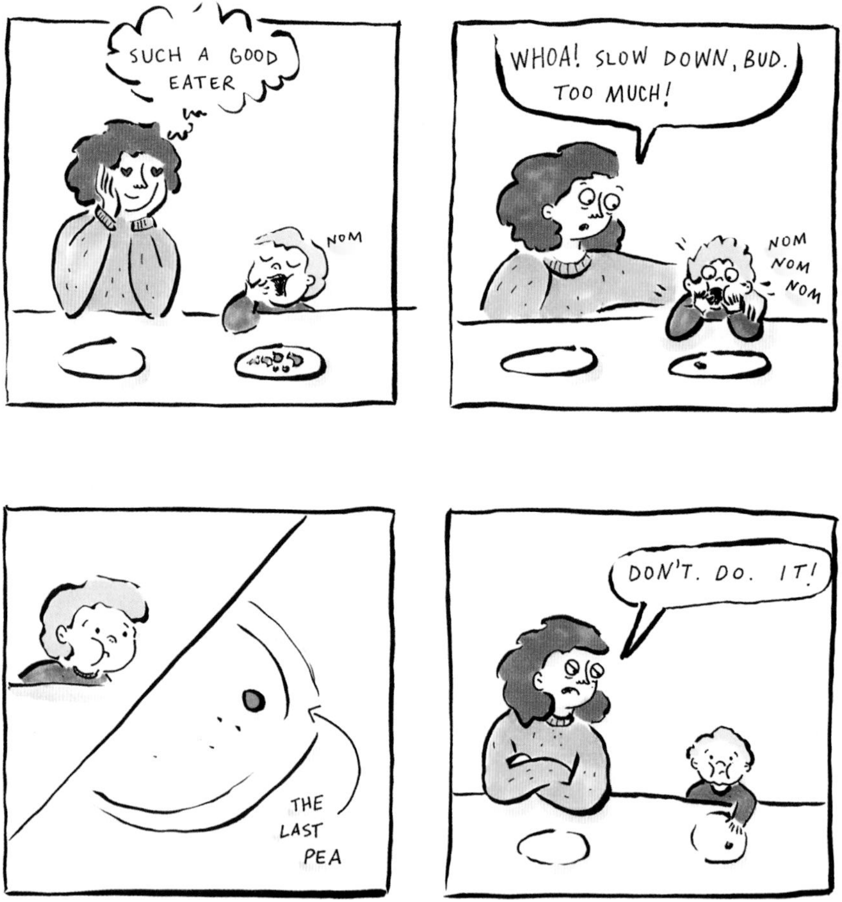
SUCH A GOOD EATER
NOM
WHOA! SLOW DOWN, BUD. TOO MUCH!
NOM NOM NOM
THE LAST PEA
DON'T. DO. IT!

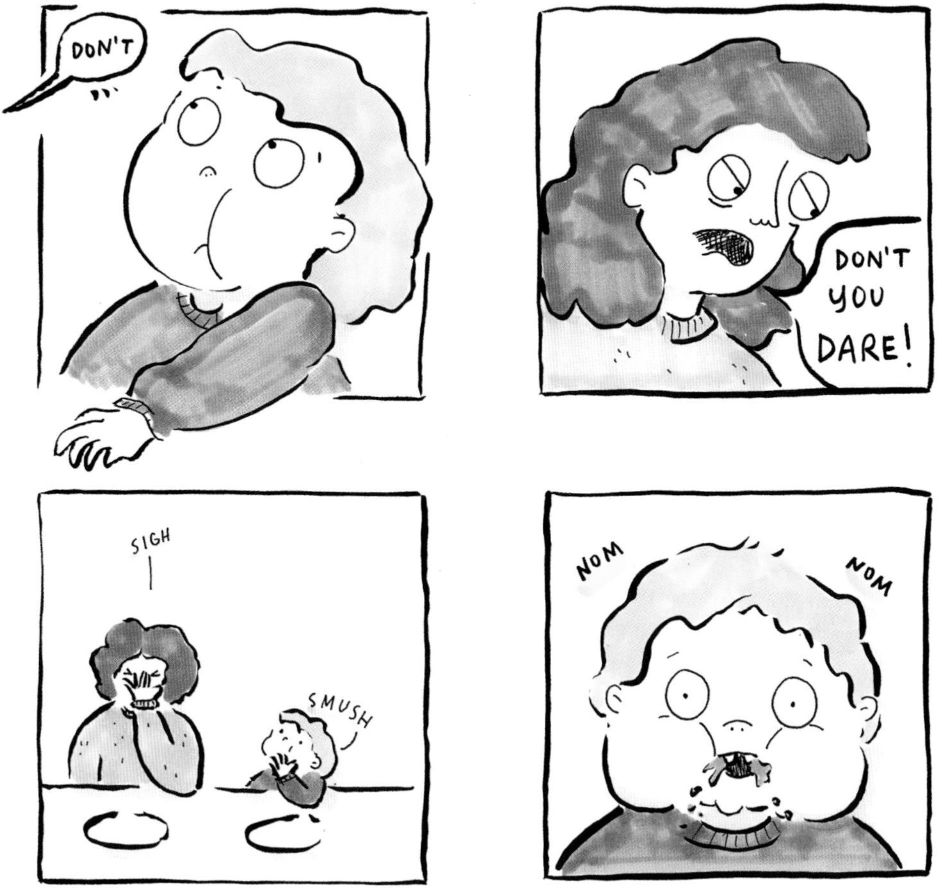
DON'T
DON'T YOU DARE!
SIGH
SMUSH
NOM
NOM

THINGS I SAID WHEN I WAS TIRED...

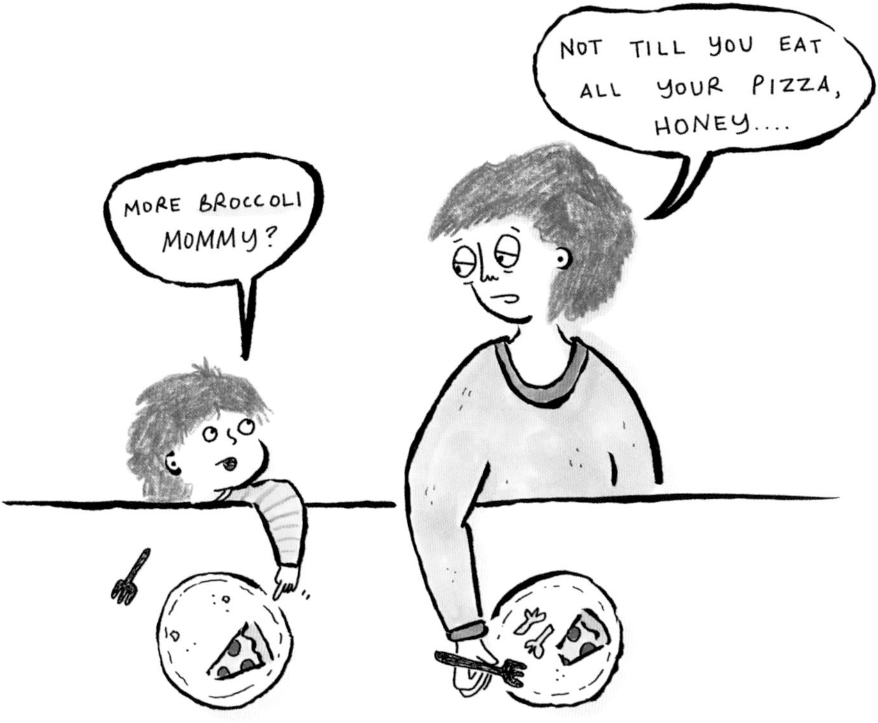
MORE BROCCOLI MOMMY?
NOT TILL YOU EAT ALL YOUR PIZZA, HONEY....

COFFEE GEOLOGY

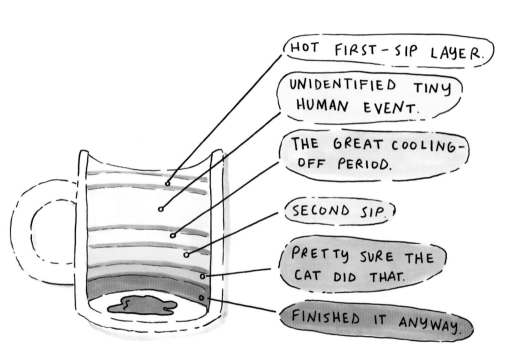

HOT FIRST-SIP LAYER.

UNIDENTIFIED TINY HUMAN EVENT.

THE GREAT COOLING-OFF PERIOD.

SECOND SIP.

PRETTY SURE THE CAT DID THAT.

FINISHED IT ANYWAY.

THE BEGINNING OF A BEAUTIFUL FRIENDSHIP

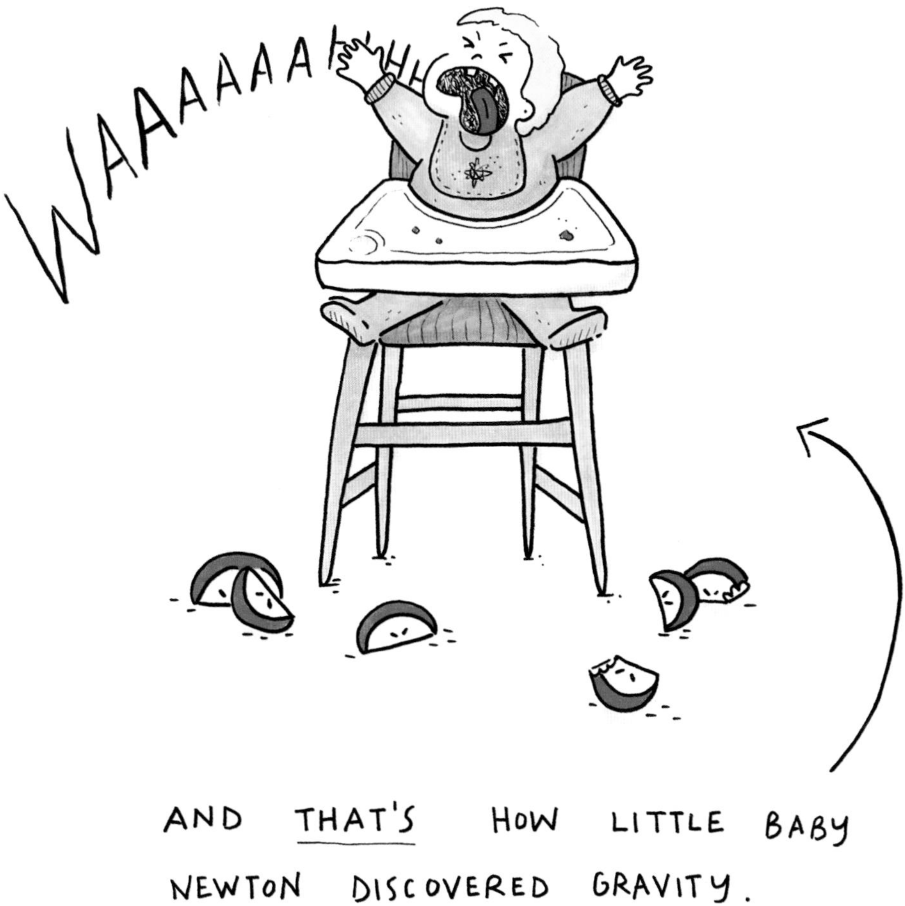
WAAAAAAAHHH

AND THAT'S HOW LITTLE BABY NEWTON DISCOVERED GRAVITY.

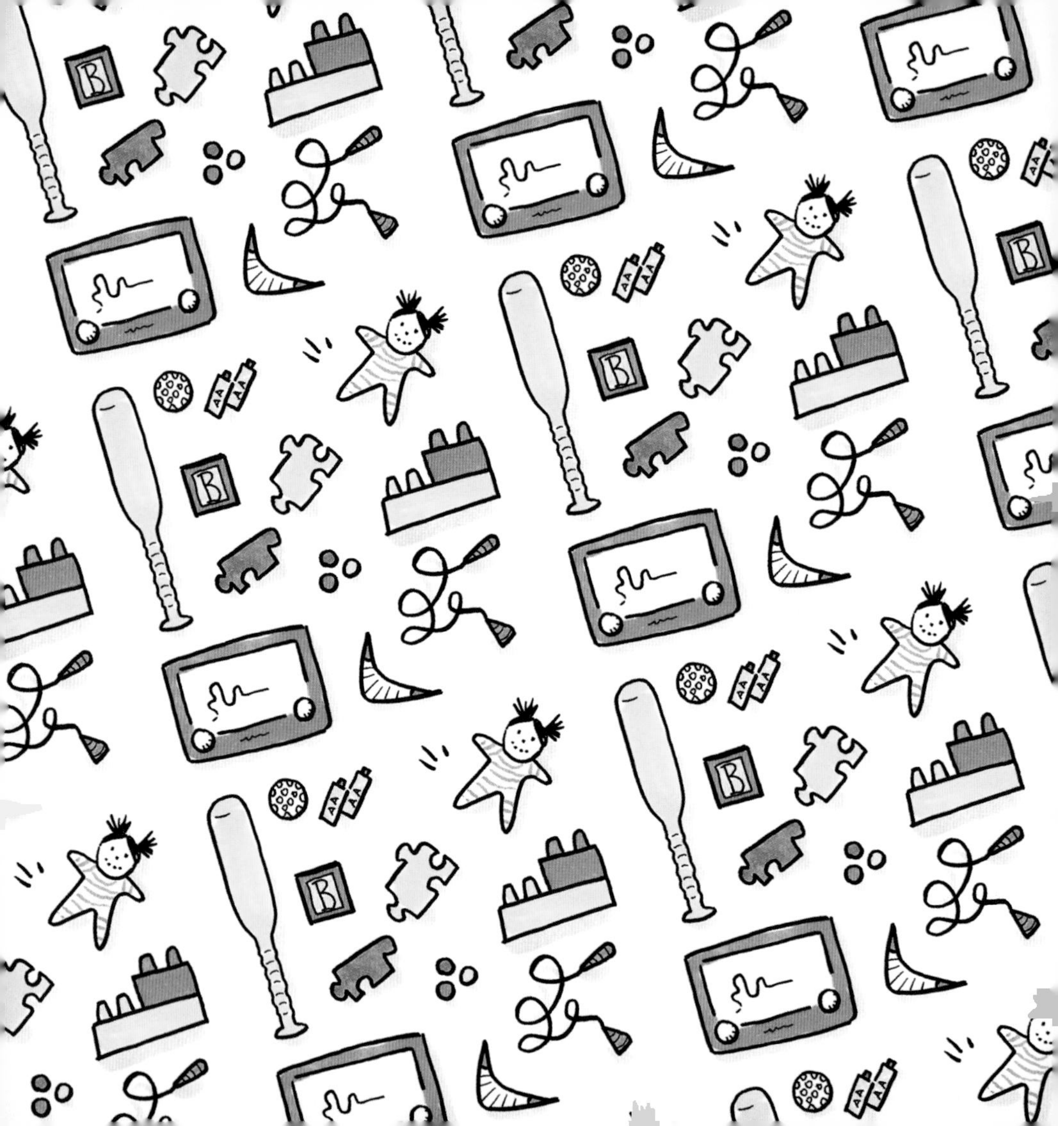

4

PLAY DAZE

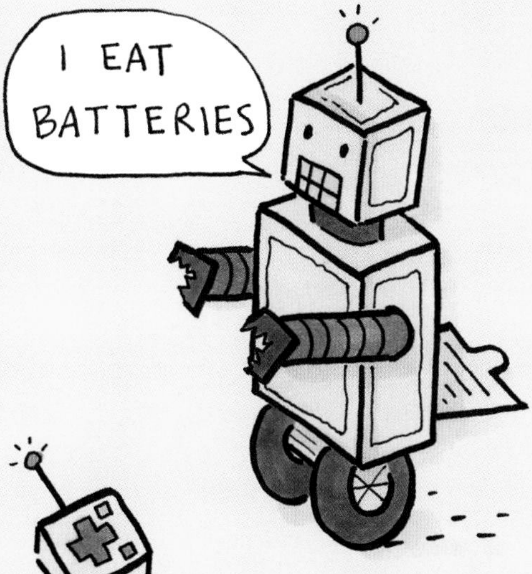
I EAT BATTERIES

THE BOUGIE BABY TOY GUIDE

THE "SINGLE PIECE" PUZZLE

$85

PERFECT FOR THE MINIMALIST BABY.

THAT GIANT KNOT THINGY

SO SOFT!

$101

THESE ARTISANAL BLOCKS

$96

SET OF FOUR. NO MORE. NO LESS.

AN IMITATION TISSUE BOX

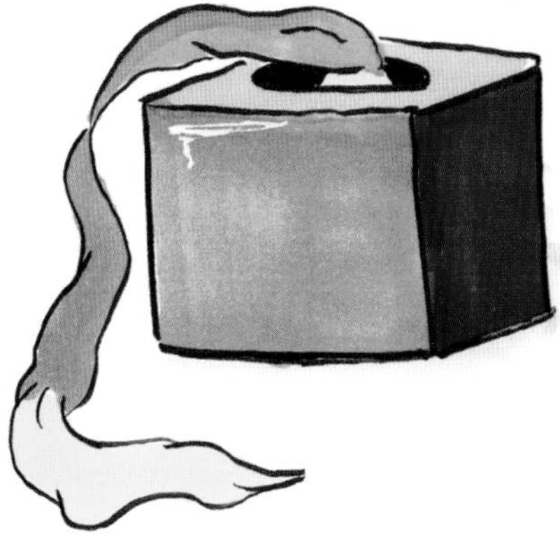

PRACTICE FOR WHEN BABY SEES A REAL TISSUE BOX FOR THE FIRST TIME.

$150–

A BESPOKE WOODEN RING TEETHER

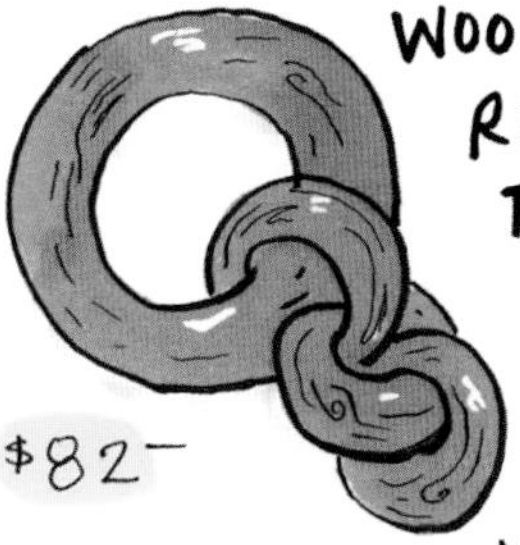

$82–

YOUR CHILD WILL NEVER ACTUALLY USE THIS.

THIS DECK OF CARDS

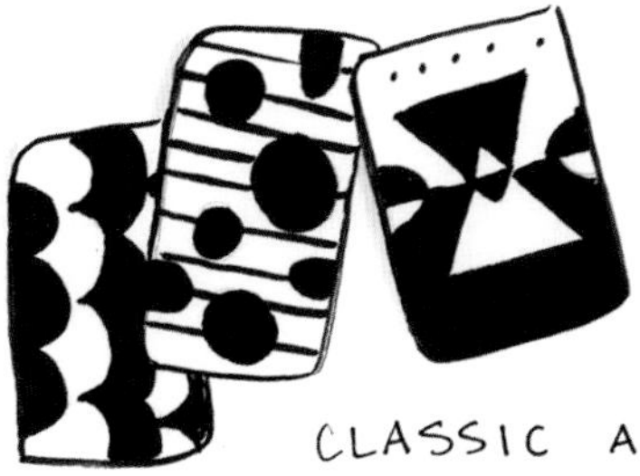

CLASSIC AND UNDERSTATED.

$75–

PLAYING HIDE 'N' SEEK WITH A BABY.

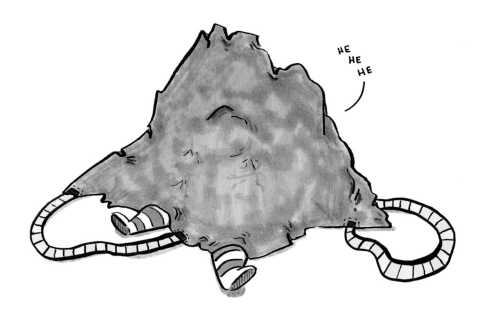

KEYS SONG

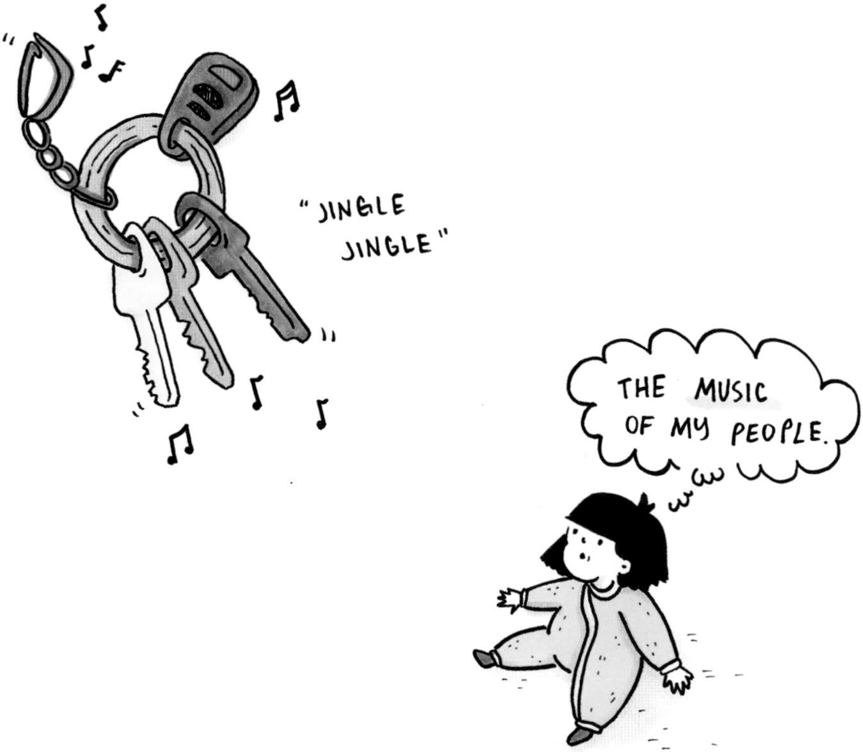
"JINGLE
JINGLE"
THE MUSIC
OF MY PEOPLE.

LET'S PLAY OUTSIDE

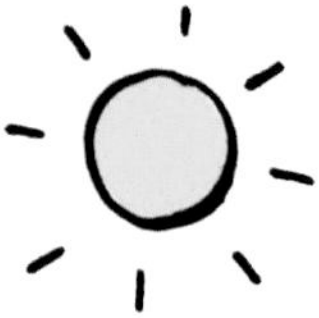

TOO BRIGHT

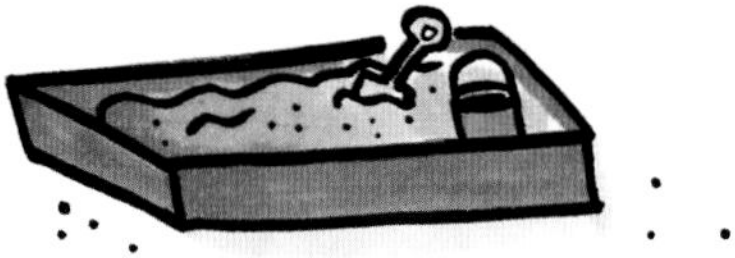

TOO DIRTY

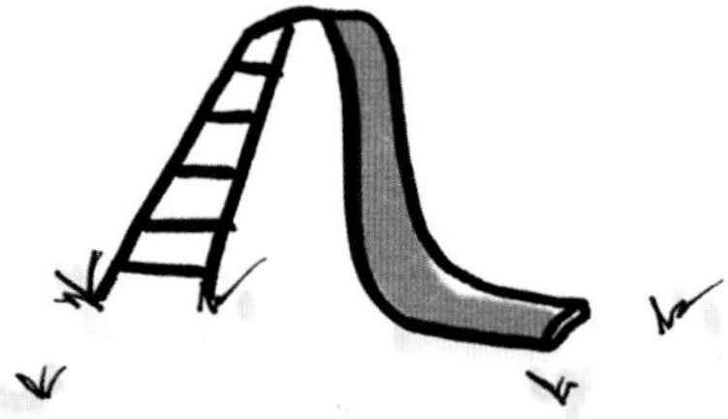

TOO HIGH

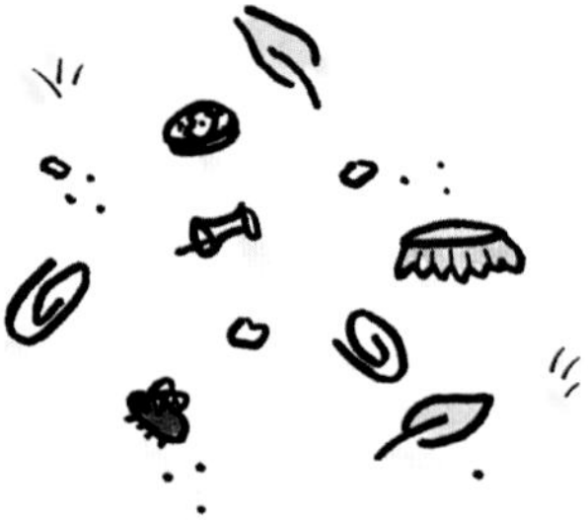

TOO SMALL

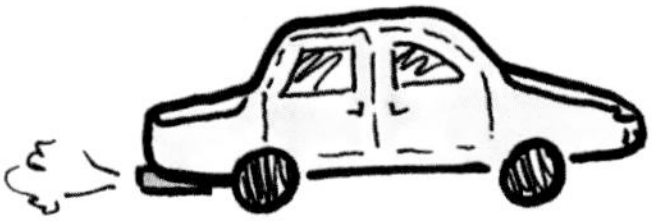

TOO FAST

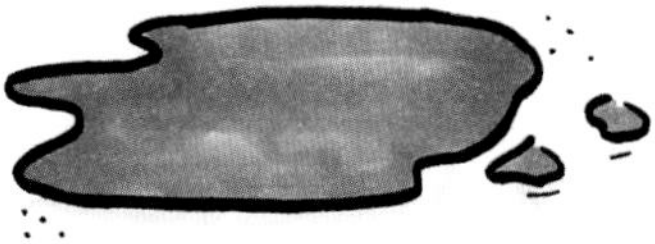

TOO WET

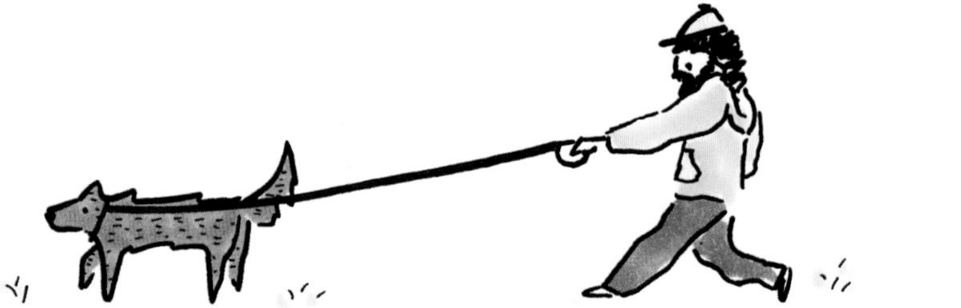

TOO FURRY

ALSO TOO FURRY

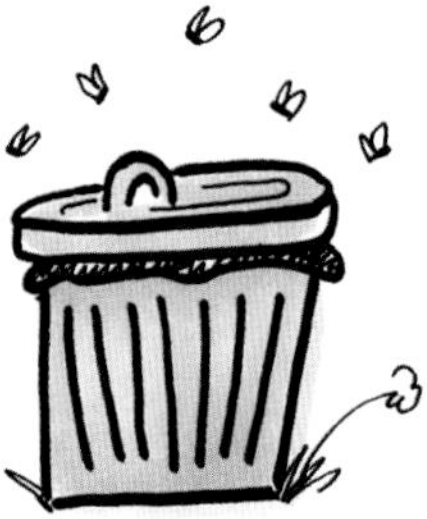

TOO GROSS

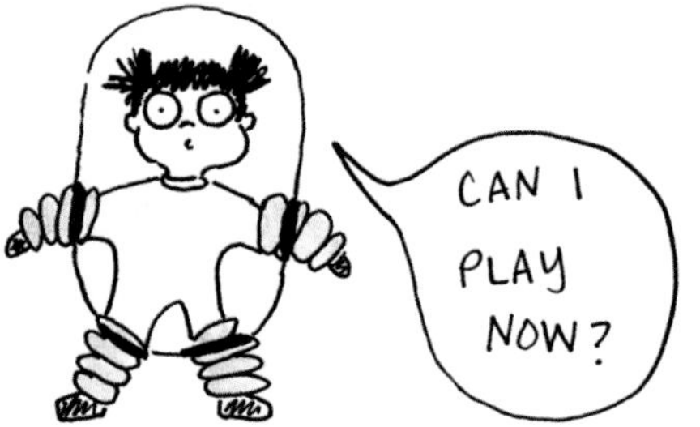
CAN I PLAY NOW?

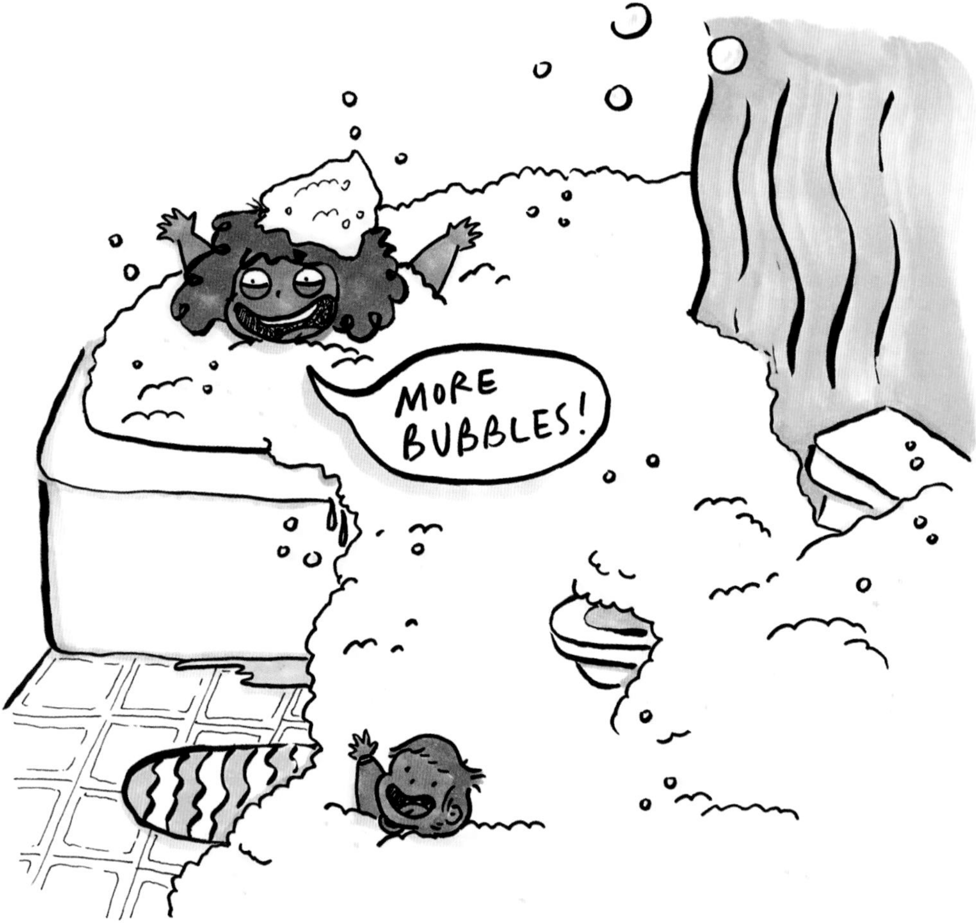
MORE BUBBLES!

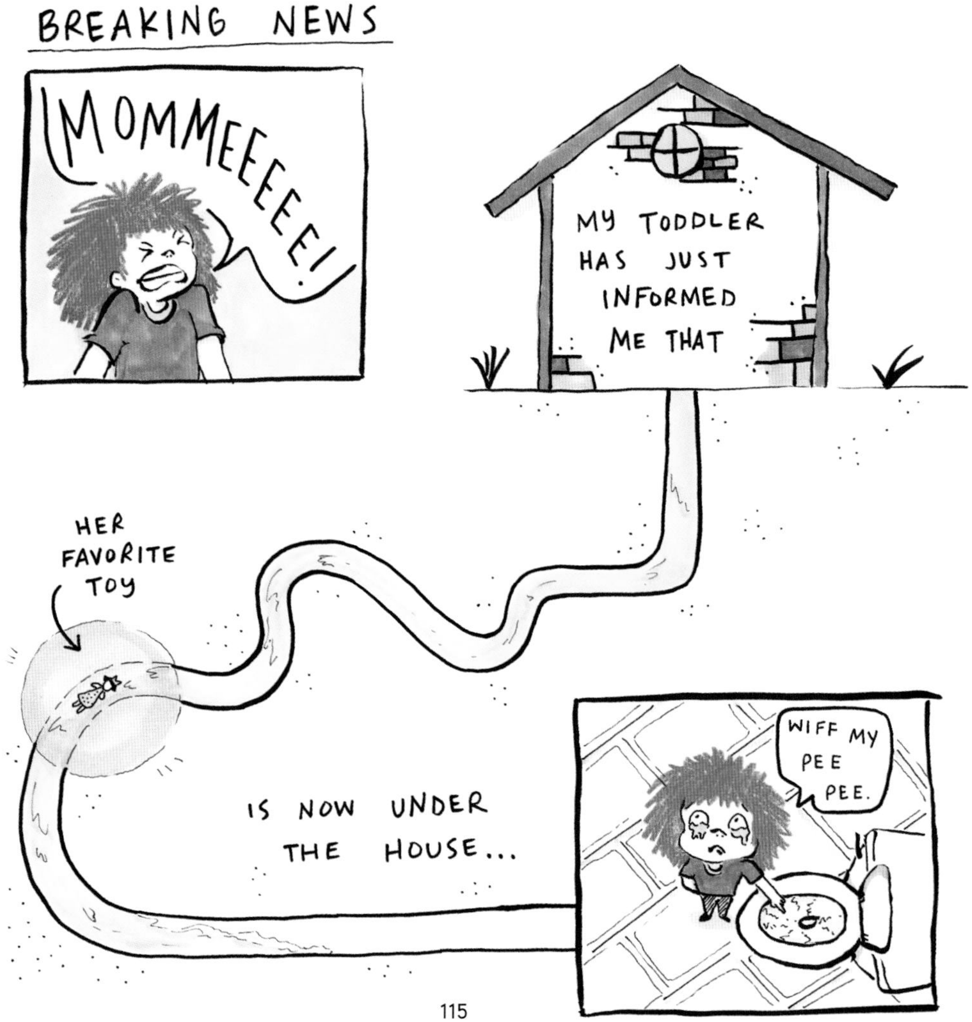
BREAKING NEWS
MOMMEEEEEE!
MY TODDLER HAS JUST INFORMED ME THAT
HER FAVORITE TOY
IS NOW UNDER THE HOUSE...
WIFF MY PEE PEE.

THE TROUBLE WITH PLAY DATES: PRETENDING

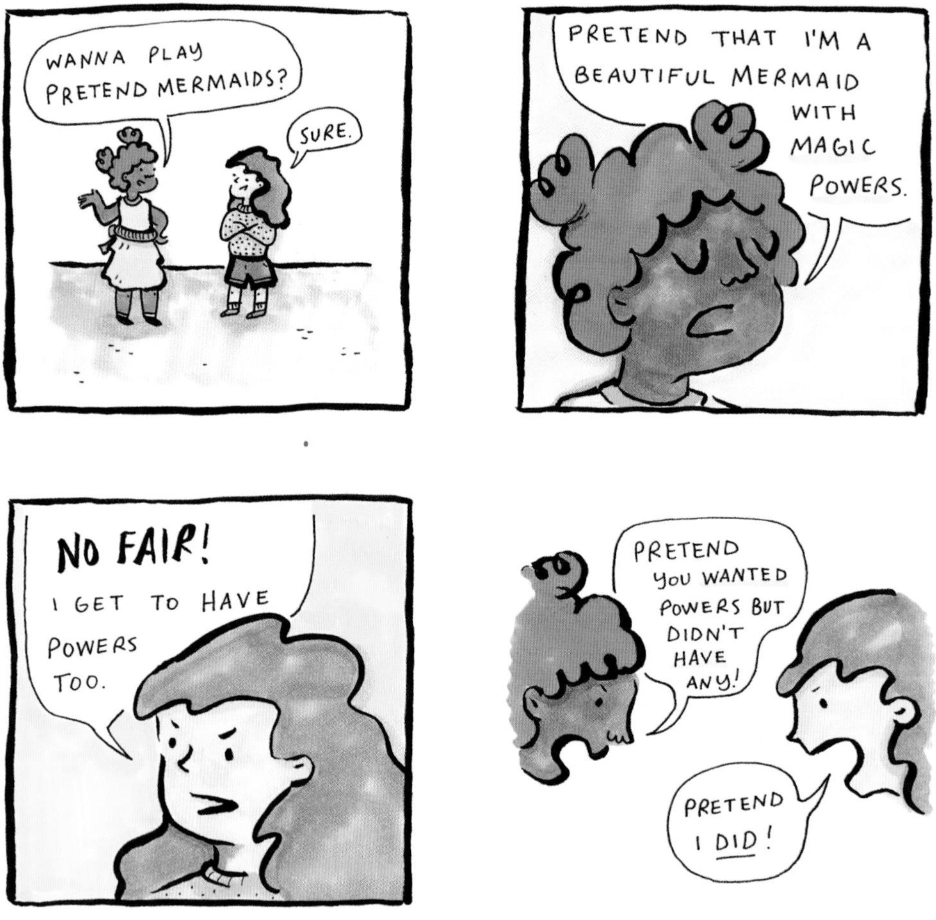
WANNA PLAY PRETEND MERMAIDS?
SURE.
PRETEND THAT I'M A BEAUTIFUL MERMAID WITH MAGIC POWERS.
NO FAIR! I GET TO HAVE POWERS TOO.
PRETEND YOU WANTED POWERS BUT DIDN'T HAVE ANY!
PRETEND I DID!

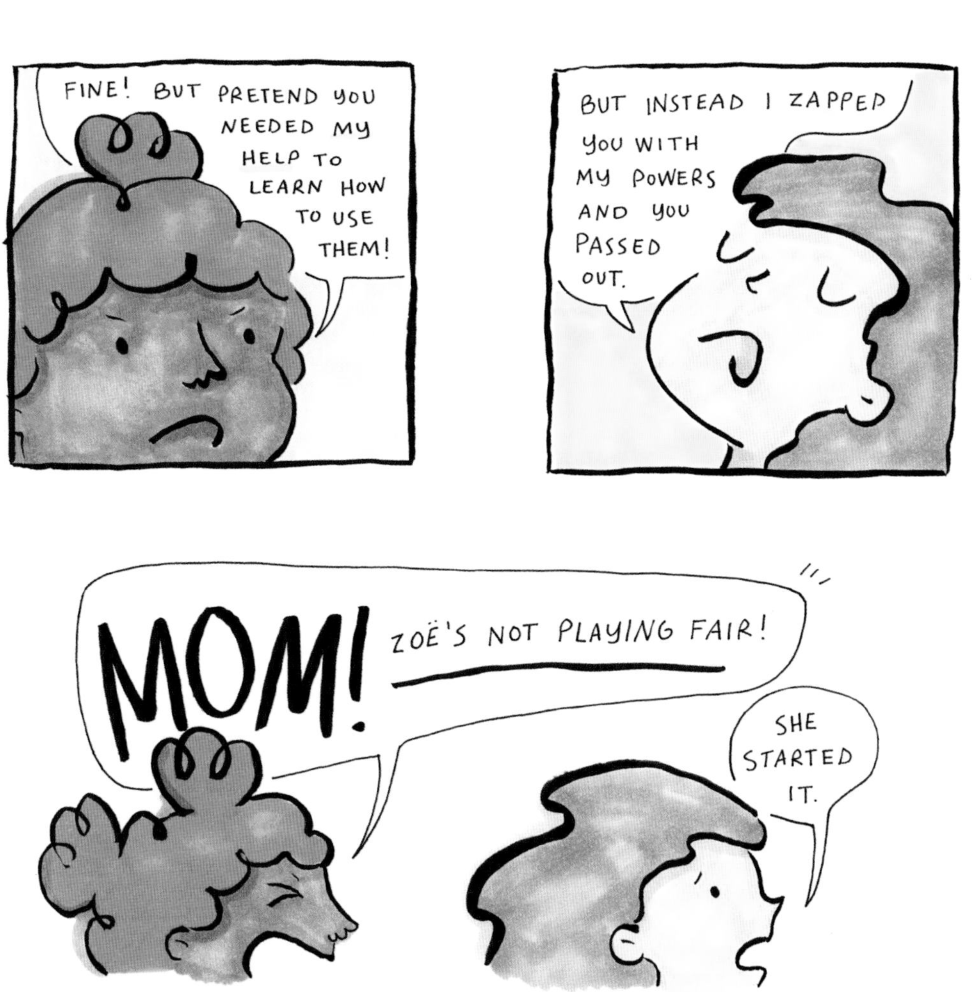
FINE! BUT PRETEND YOU NEEDED MY HELP TO LEARN HOW TO USE THEM!
BUT INSTEAD I ZAPPED YOU WITH MY POWERS AND YOU PASSED OUT.
MOM! ZOË'S NOT PLAYING FAIR!
SHE STARTED IT.

SENSORY BIN?

OF COURSE MY
CHILD HAS A
"SENSORY BIN" FULL OF
CAREFULLY CURATED
AGE-APPROPRIATE STIMULI

AND WE REFILL IT
EVERY WEEK!

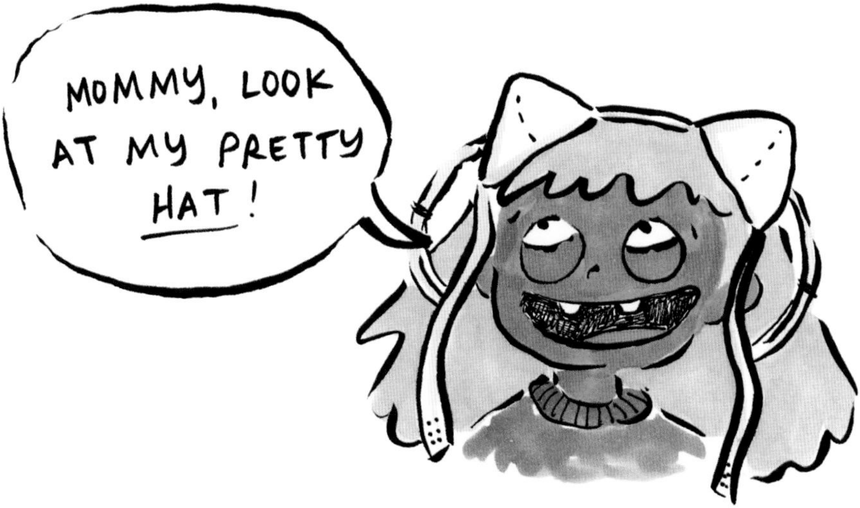
MOMMY, LOOK AT MY PRETTY HAT!

NOTHING IS SACRED IN MOMMYHOOD

WHAT IS MY TODDLER THINKING?

"I CAN STAND ON THAT."

A BOX
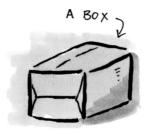

"I SHOULD STAND ON THAT."

A BOWL

"STILL CAN'T STAND ON THAT."

A SIPPY CUP

"TRYING TO STAND ON THAT RIGHT NOW."

A BALL

"DEFINITELY GOING TO STAND ON THAT."

THIS UPSIDE-DOWN THING

THE CAT

"DON'T MOVE SO I CAN STAND ON YOU."

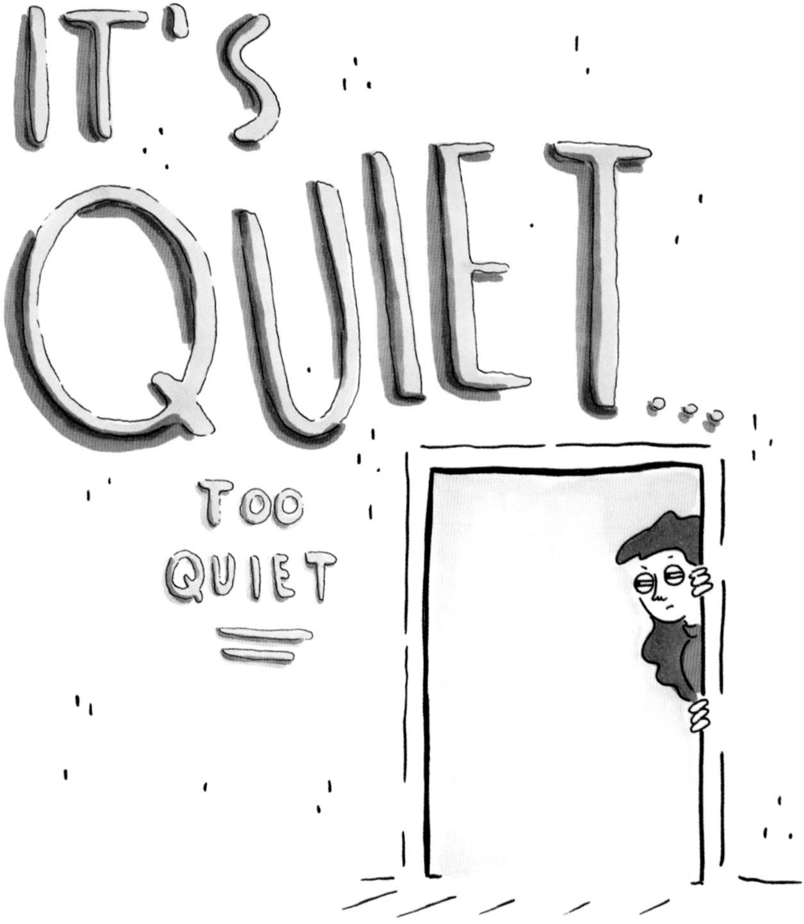
IT'S QUIET...
TOO QUIET

"MOM! LOOK! I MADE A BEAUTIFUL WATERFALL."

RAINBOW UNICORN BIRTHDAY PARTY

INSPIRATION

UNICORN CAKE

TASTEFUL RAINBOW DECOR

RAINBOW LAND BOUNCY CASTLE

UNICORN PIÑATA

CHARMING PARTY SNACKS

(TOTAL COST) = A SEMESTER OF FUTURE COLLEGE TUITION

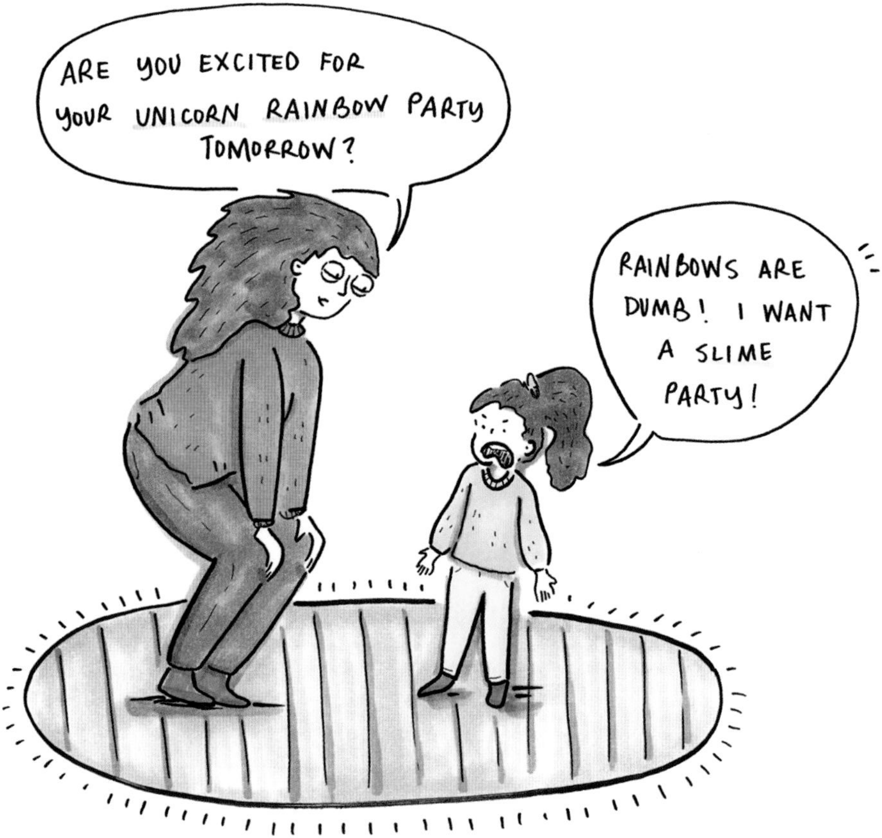
ARE YOU EXCITED FOR YOUR UNICORN RAINBOW PARTY TOMORROW?
RAINBOWS ARE DUMB! I WANT A SLIME PARTY!

EVERYONE ELSE'S TODDLER

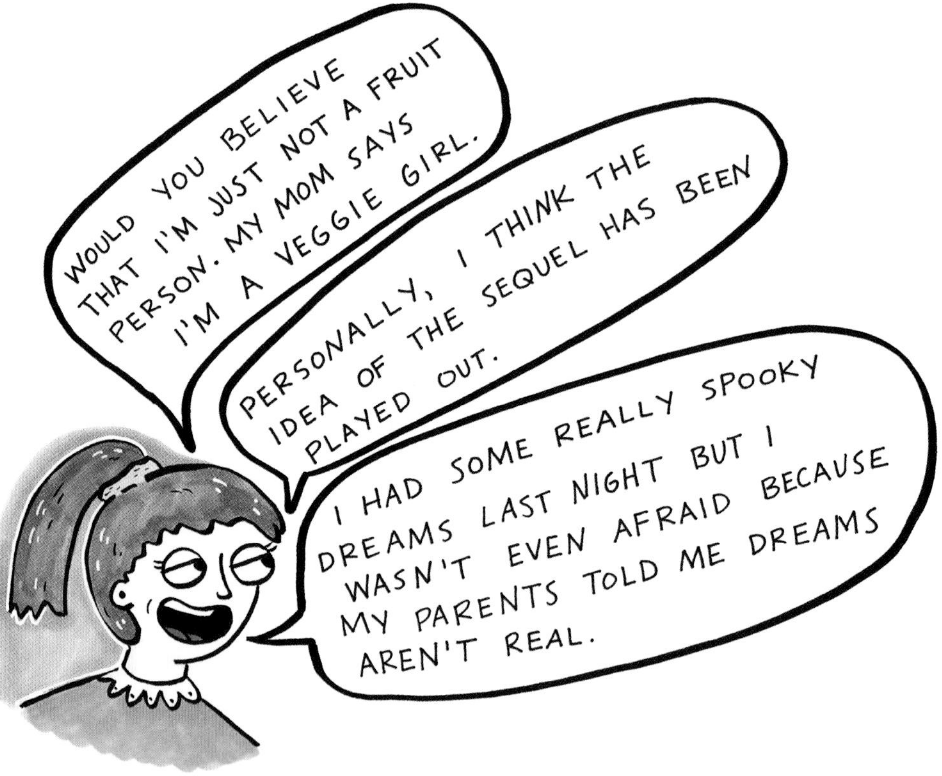
WOULD YOU BELIEVE THAT I'M JUST NOT A FRUIT PERSON. MY MOM SAYS I'M A VEGGIE GIRL.
PERSONALLY, I THINK THE IDEA OF THE SEQUEL HAS BEEN PLAYED OUT.
I HAD SOME REALLY SPOOKY DREAMS LAST NIGHT BUT I WASN'T EVEN AFRAID BECAUSE MY PARENTS TOLD ME DREAMS AREN'T REAL.

MY TODDLER

I WANT GREEN CUP
I WANT GREEN CUP
I WANT GREEN CUP
I WANT GREEN CUP
I WANT GREEN CUP
I WANT GREEN CUP
I WANT GREEN CUP

RESTAURANTS HAVE THE BEST TOYS!

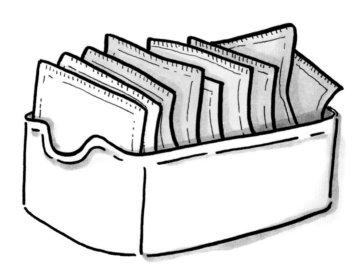

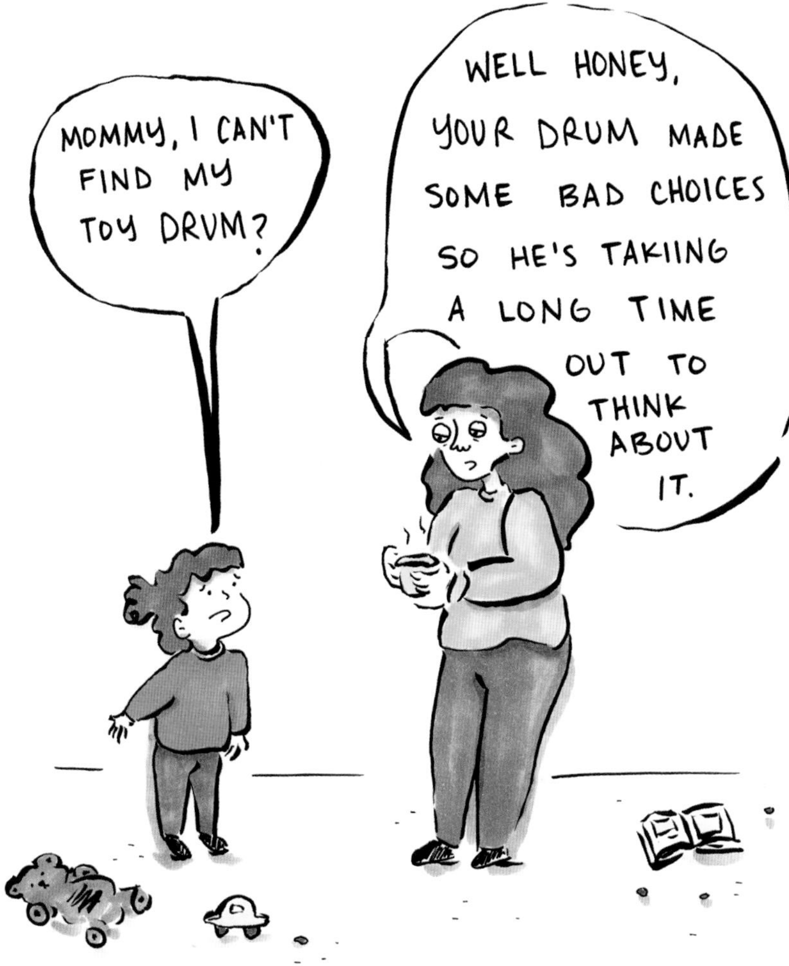
MOMMY, I CAN'T FIND MY TOY DRUM?
WELL HONEY, YOUR DRUM MADE SOME BAD CHOICES SO HE'S TAKIING A LONG TIME OUT TO THINK ABOUT IT.

THE TROUBLE WITH PLAY DATES: SNACKTIME

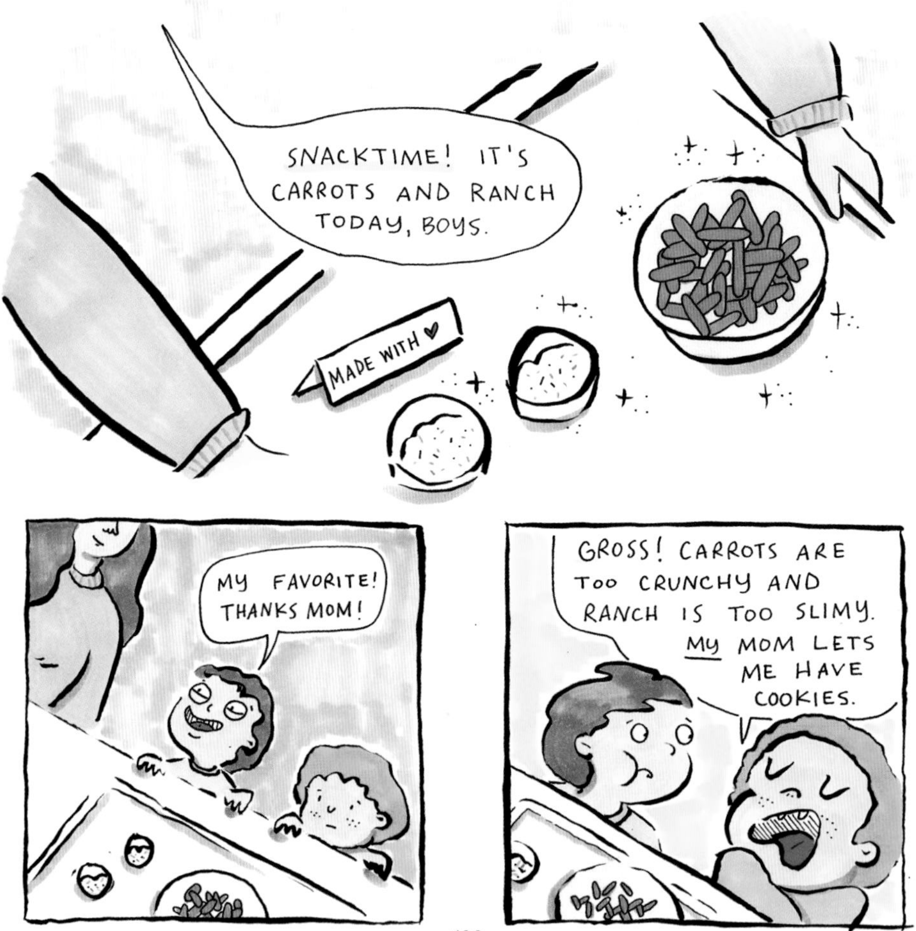
SNACKTIME! IT'S CARROTS AND RANCH TODAY, BOYS.
MADE WITH ♥
MY FAVORITE! THANKS MOM!
GROSS! CARROTS ARE TOO CRUNCHY AND RANCH IS TOO SLIMY. MY MOM LETS ME HAVE COOKIES.

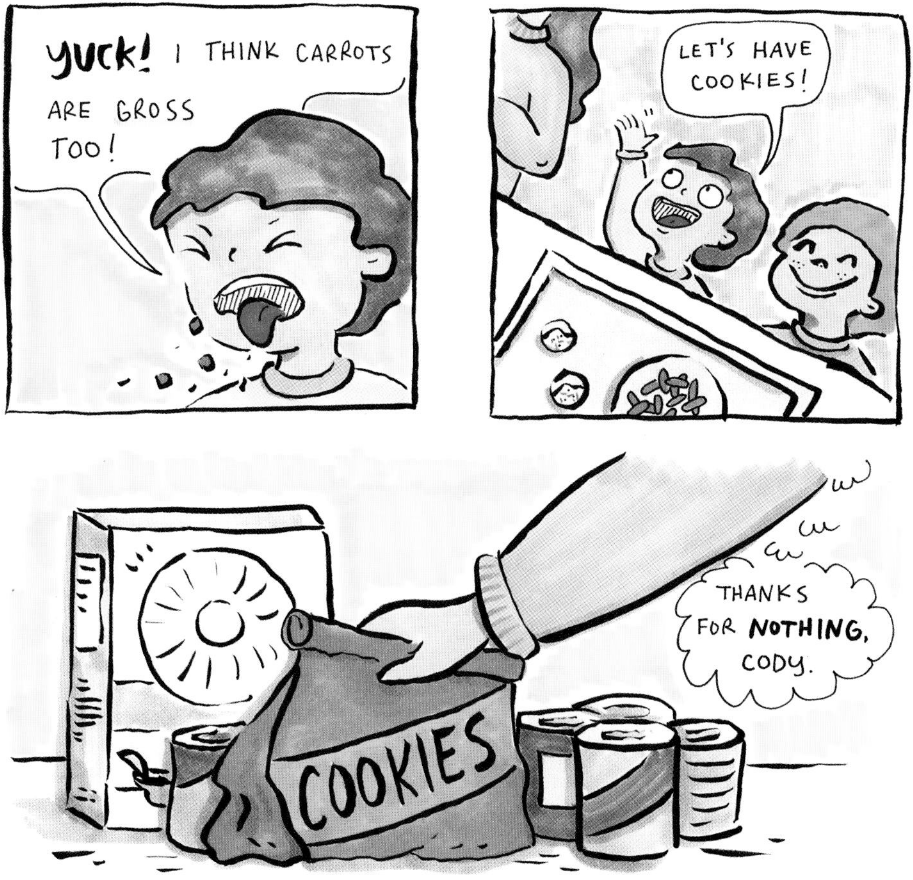
YUCK! I THINK CARROTS ARE GROSS TOO!
LET'S HAVE COOKIES!
THANKS FOR NOTHING, CODY.
COOKIES

THE INEVITABILITY OF A TOY BOX

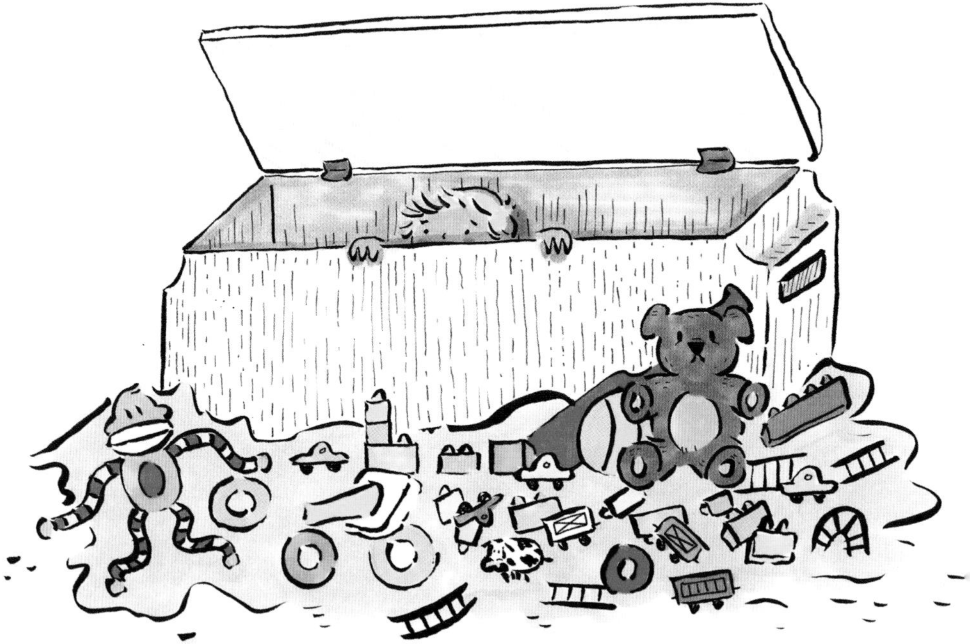

THINGS THAT ARE <u>NOT</u> A SWORD

THE BROOM

THE MOP

THIS RULER

AN OLD POOL NOODLE

THAT LONG STICK

YOUR BABY BROTHER!

TODDLER FEMINISM EXPLAINED

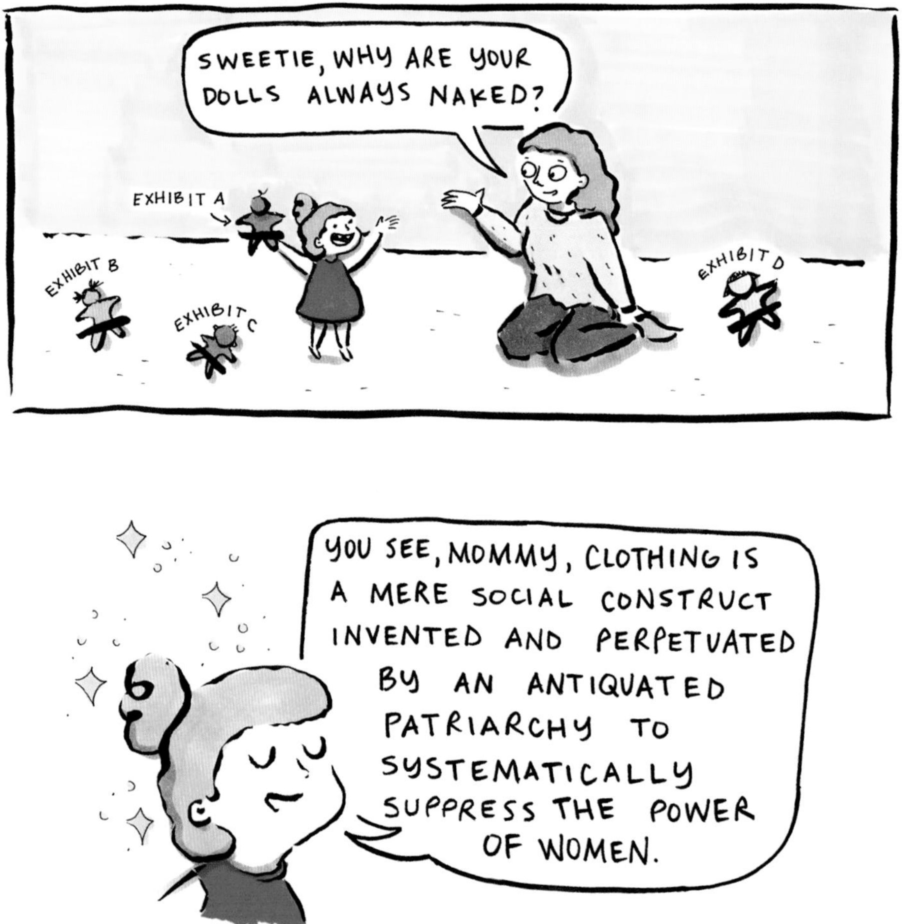

SWEETIE, WHY ARE YOUR DOLLS ALWAYS NAKED?
EXHIBIT A
EXHIBIT B
EXHIBIT C
EXHIBIT D
YOU SEE, MOMMY, CLOTHING IS A MERE SOCIAL CONSTRUCT INVENTED AND PERPETUATED BY AN ANTIQUATED PATRIARCHY TO SYSTEMATICALLY SUPPRESS THE POWER OF WOMEN.

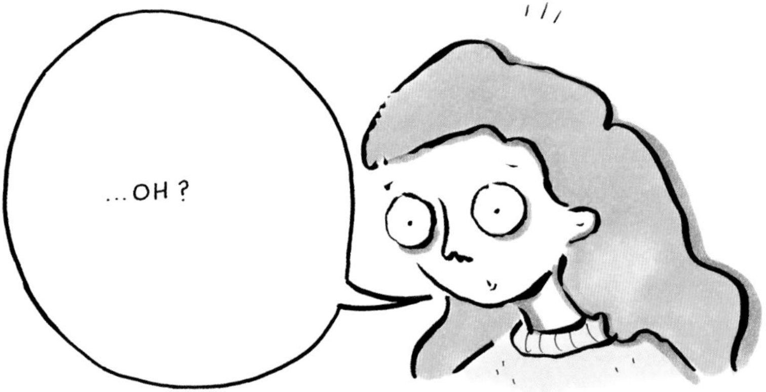
...OH ?

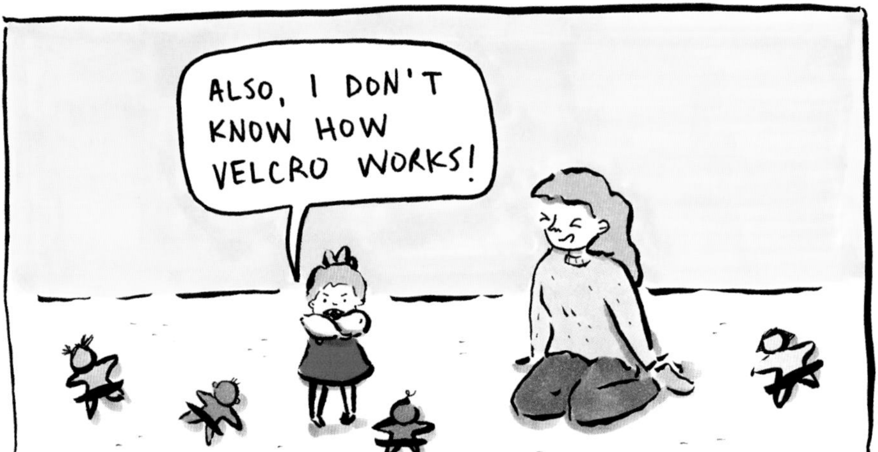
ALSO, I DON'T KNOW HOW VELCRO WORKS!

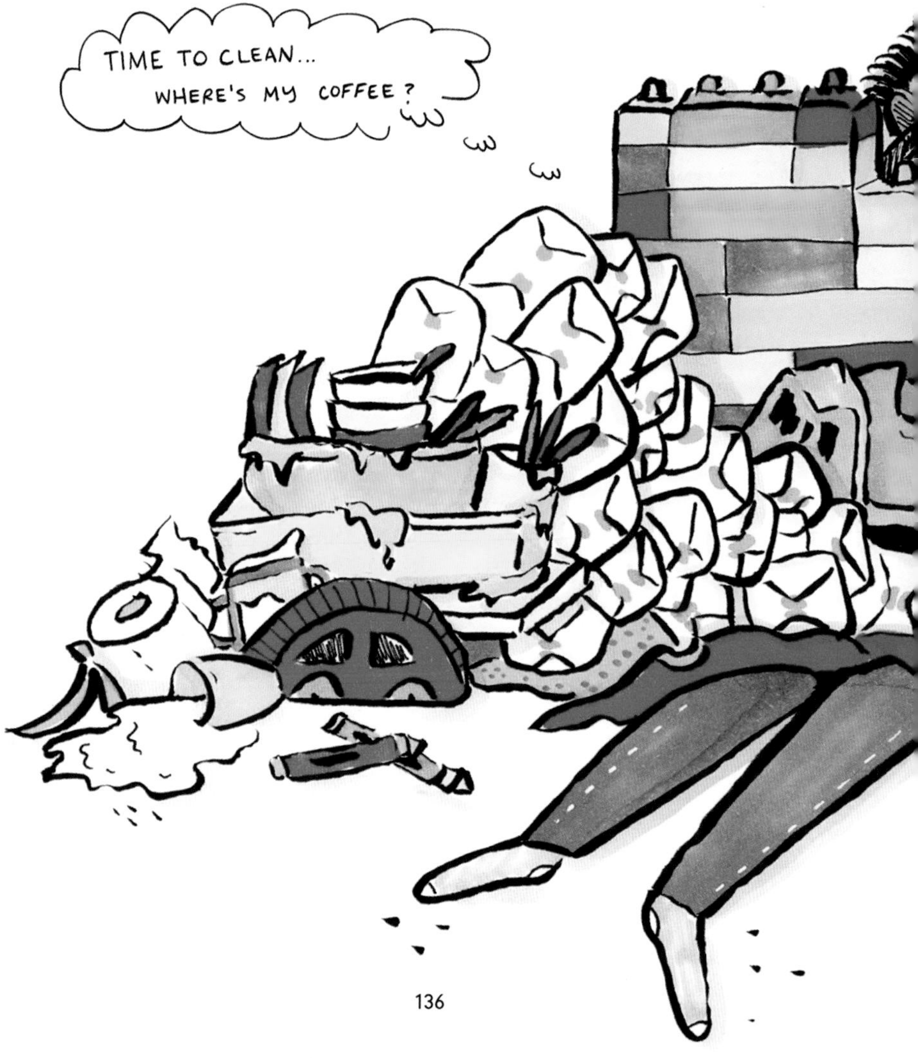
TIME TO CLEAN...
WHERE'S MY COFFEE?

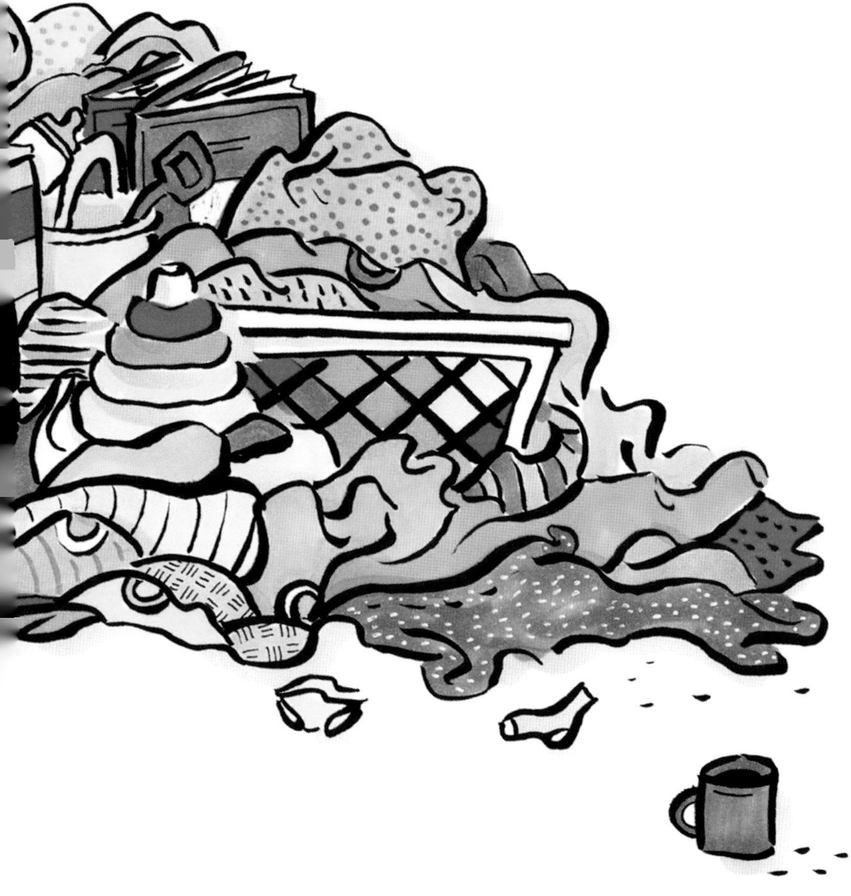

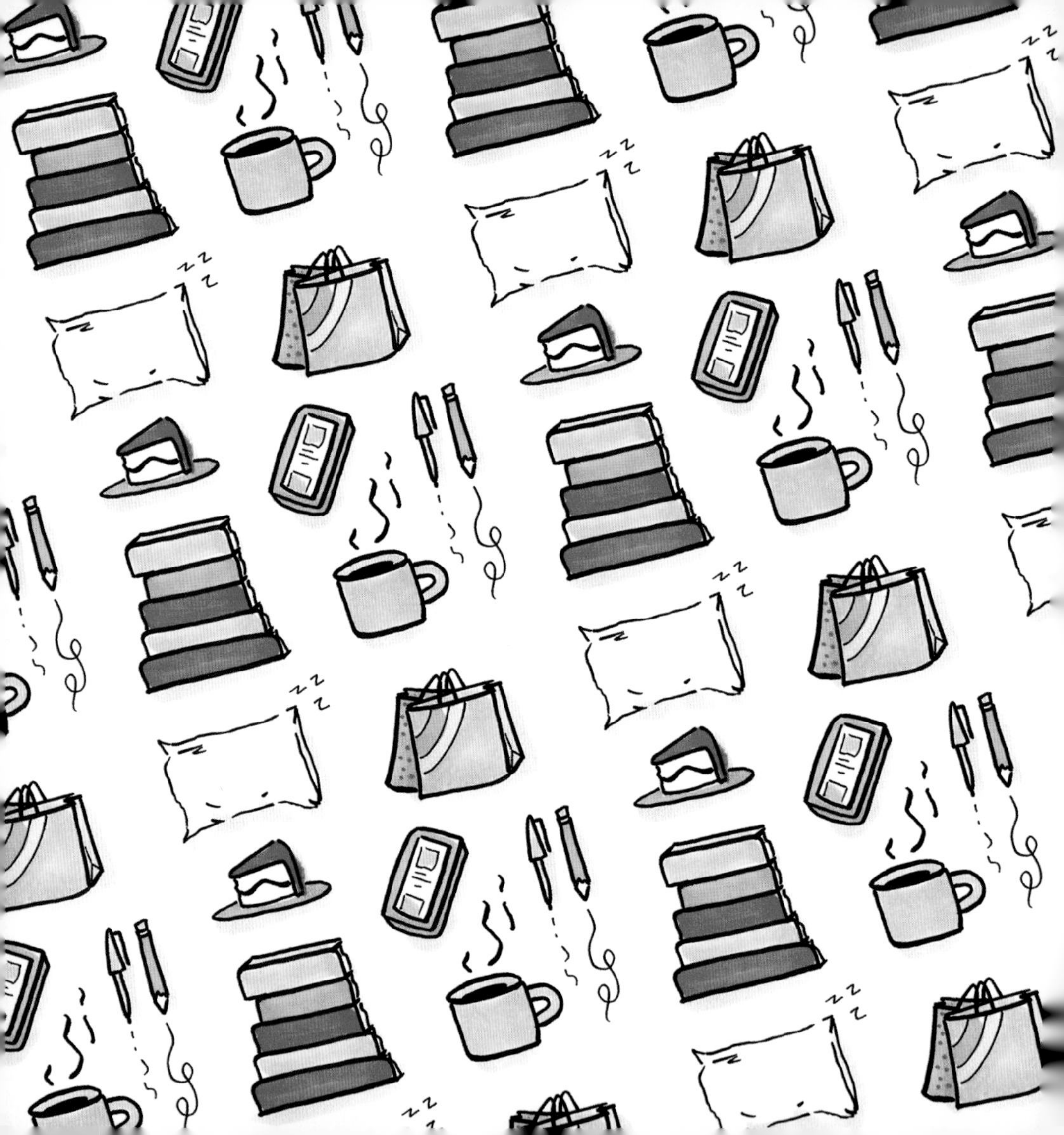

⑤

ME TIME

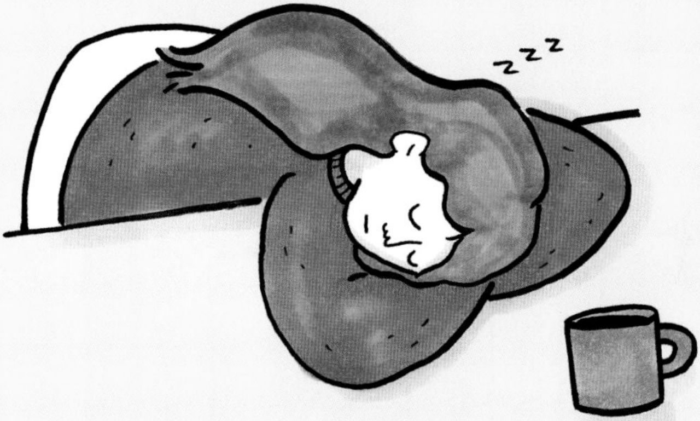

z z z

ON STRIKE

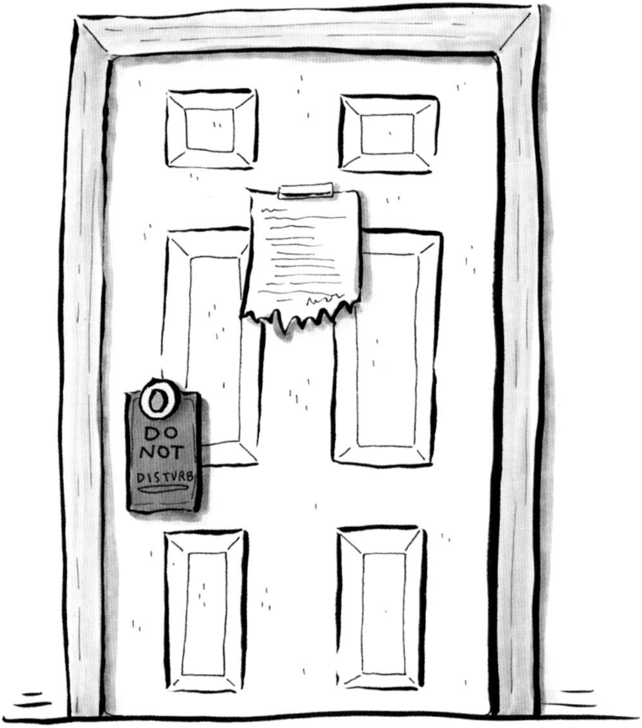
DO NOT DISTURB

DEAR FAMILY,

MOMMY IS TAKING A MUCH-NEEDED
BREAK FROM:
- CUTTING YOUR GRAPES
- CLEANING THE KITCHEN
- FOLDING YOUR UNDIES
- STEPPING ON BLOCKS
- PLAYING TEA PARTY (WITH "REAL" WATER)
- CLEANING THE KITCHEN
- READING THE SAME BOOK 100 TIMES
- CUTTING YOUR APPLES
- MAKING THREE DIFFERENT LUNCHES
- REFILLING YOUR WATER
- CLEANING UP SPILLED WATER
- CLEANING THE KITCHEN
- SINGING "THIS OLD MAN"
- CUTTING MORE STRAWBERRIES
- PICKING UP SOCKS
- ASKING "WHERE DID YOU GET THAT?"
- AND KEEPING THAT KITCHEN CLEAN!

IF YOU NEED ME FOR ANY REASON
AT ALL ... BRING CHOCOLATE.

— Mom

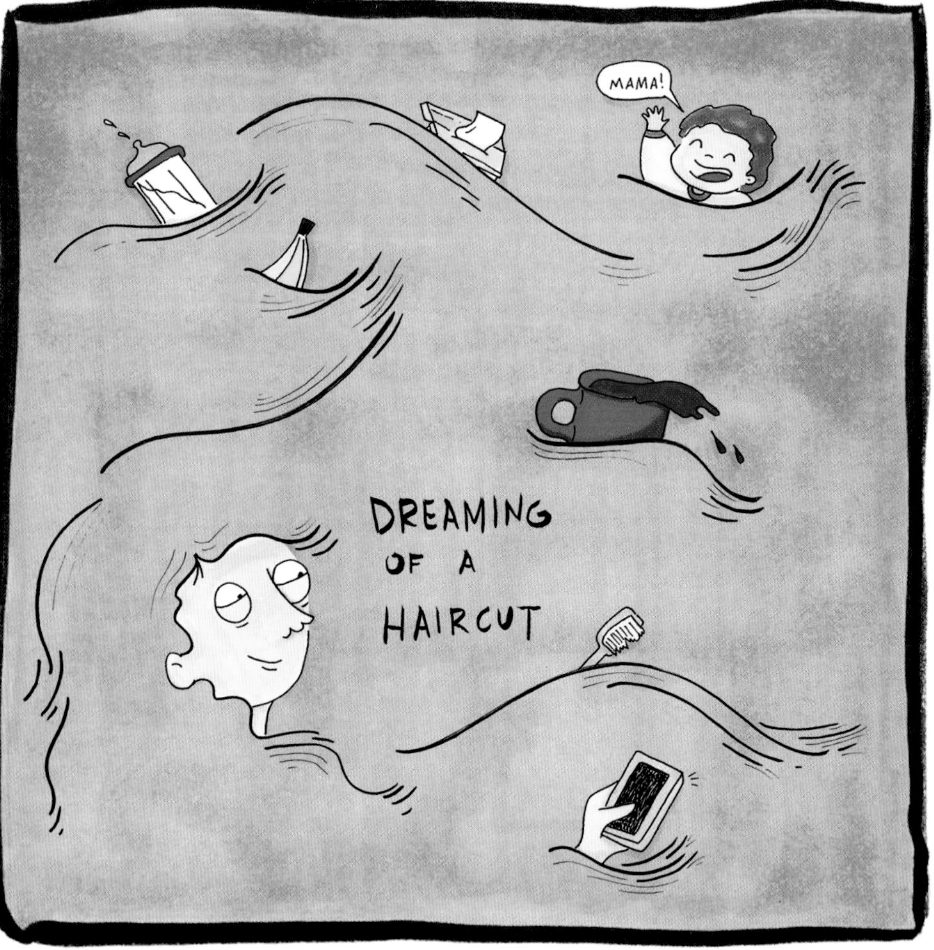
MAMA!
DREAMING OF A HAIRCUT

QUIET TIME

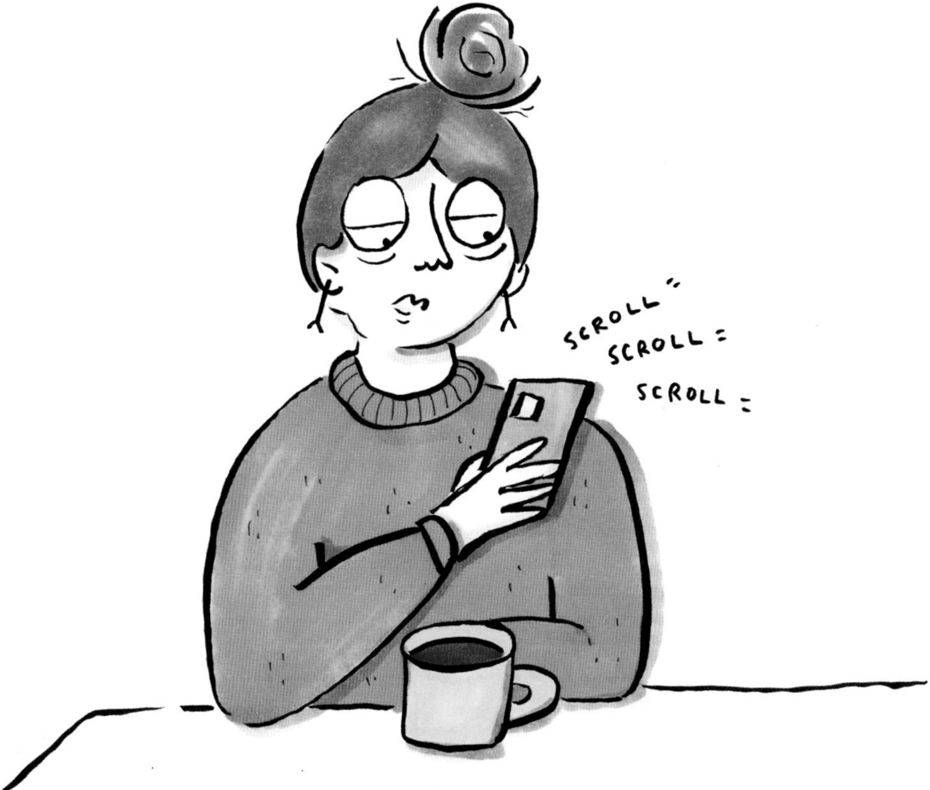
SCROLL
SCROLL
SCROLL

HOW TO FIND MORE

① LET THE LAUNDRY PILE UP

② FORGET TO SHOWER

③ DISHES? WHAT DISHES?

TIME FOR YOURSELF

④ INSTITUTE A "NO BARE FEET" RULE

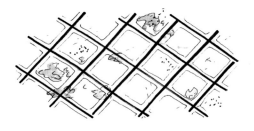

⑤ KEEP THE KIDS BUSY WITH MARGINALLY EDUCATIONAL ENTERTAINMENT

LET'S SPARKLE

I RUN ON VITAMINS AND COFFEE.

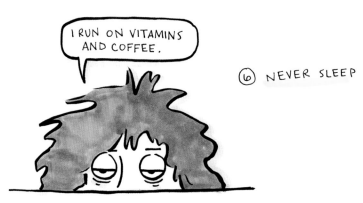

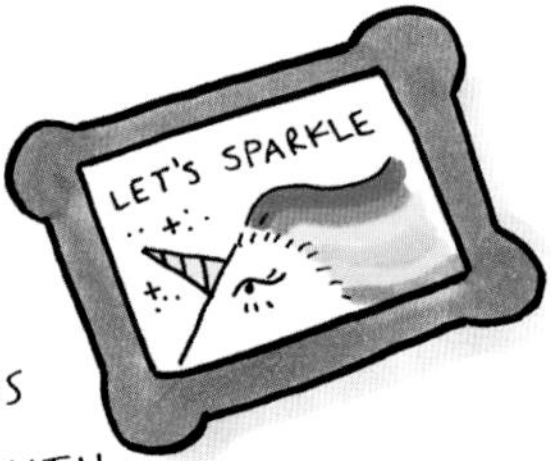

⑥ NEVER SLEEP

NIGHTMARES

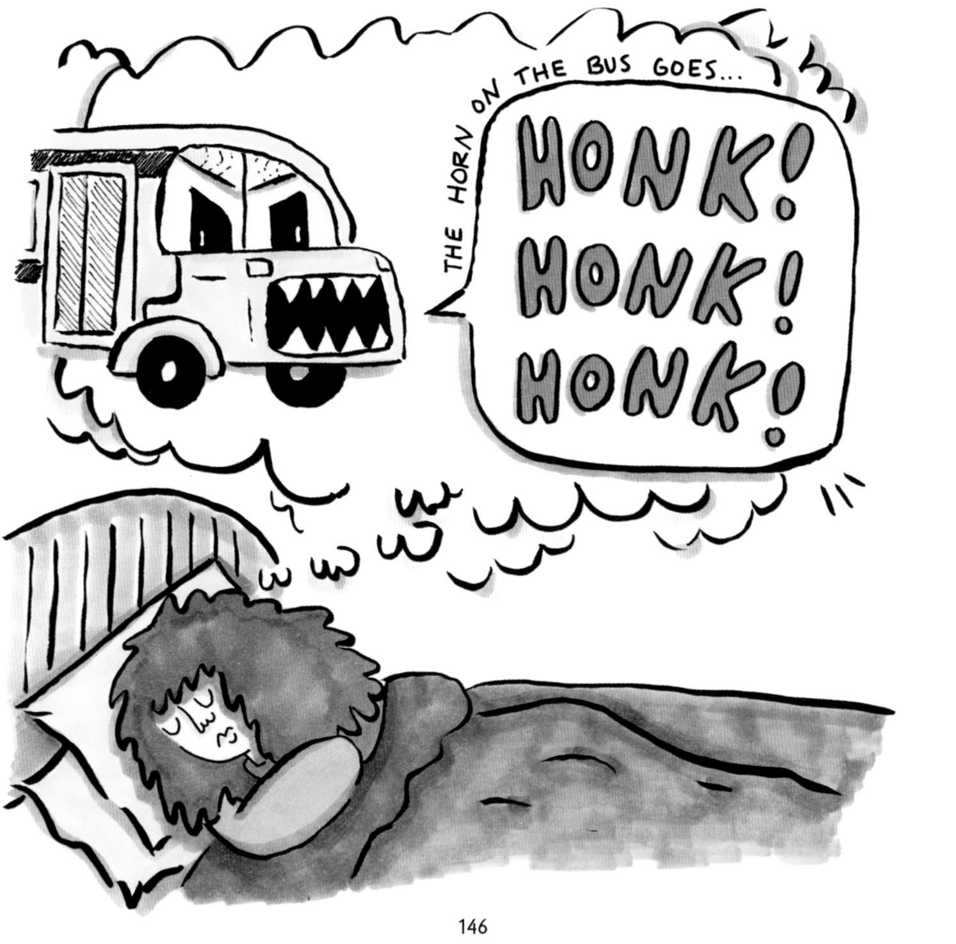
THE HORN ON THE BUS GOES...
HONK! HONK! HONK!

MIDNIGHT INTRUDER

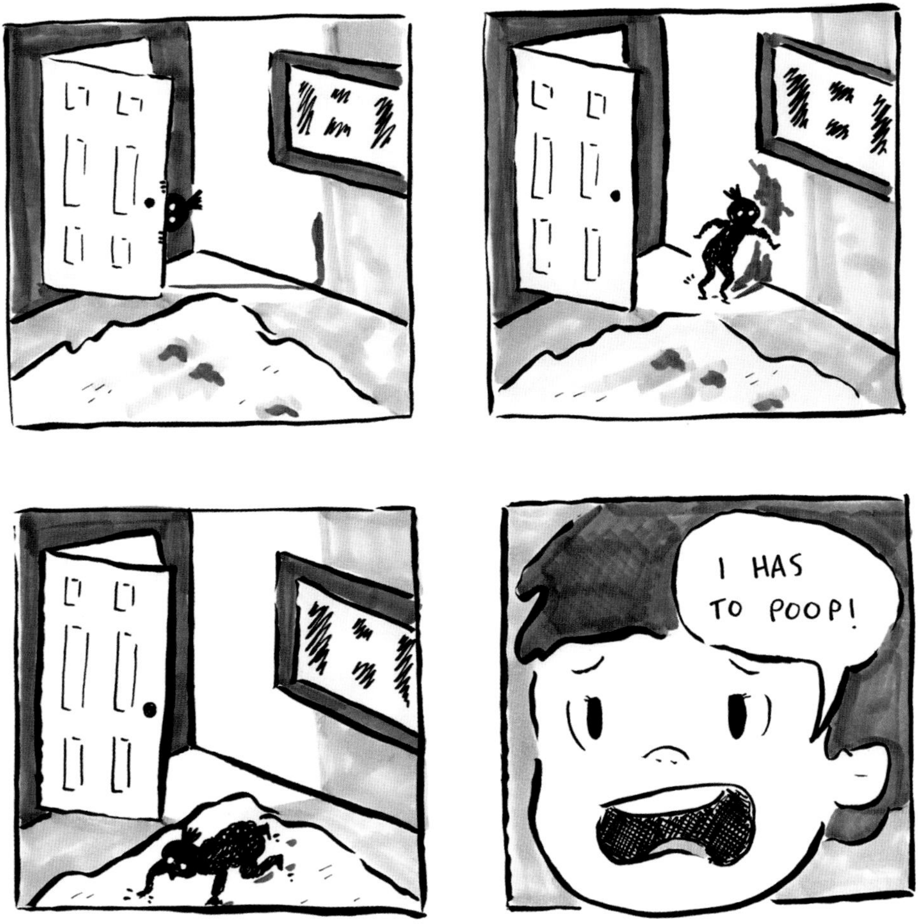
I HAS TO POOP!

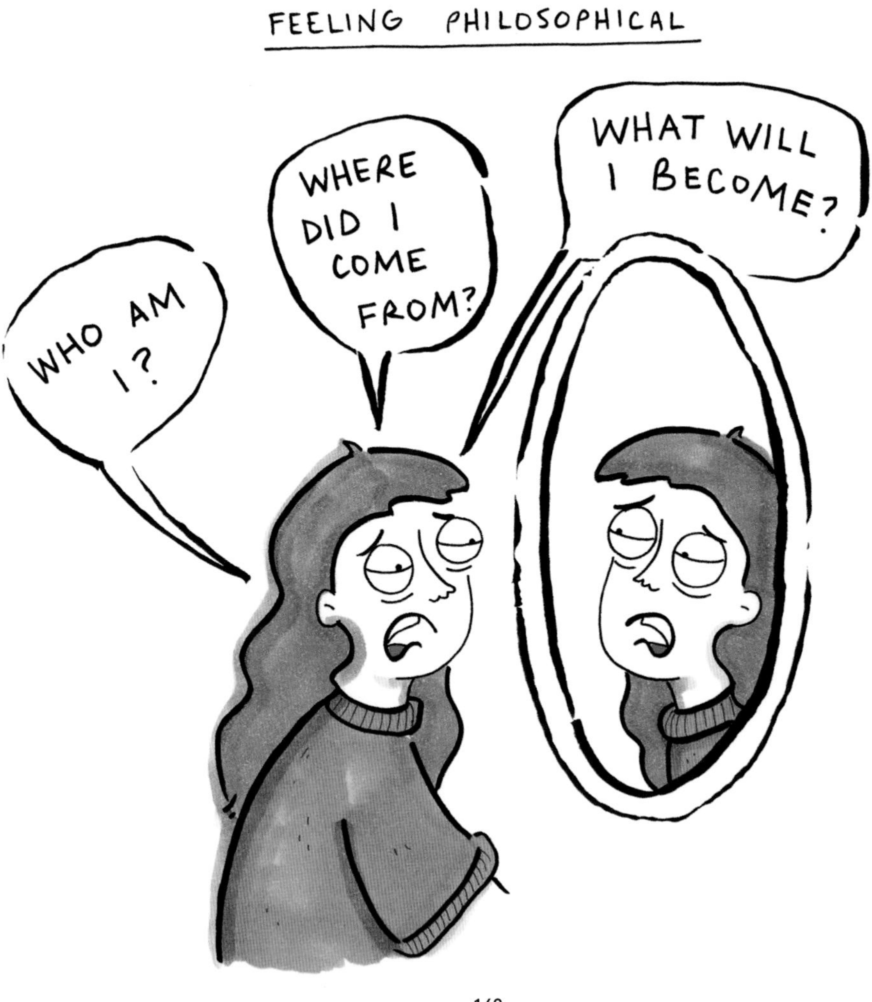
FEELING PHILOSOPHICAL
WHO AM I?
WHERE DID I COME FROM?
WHAT WILL I BECOME?

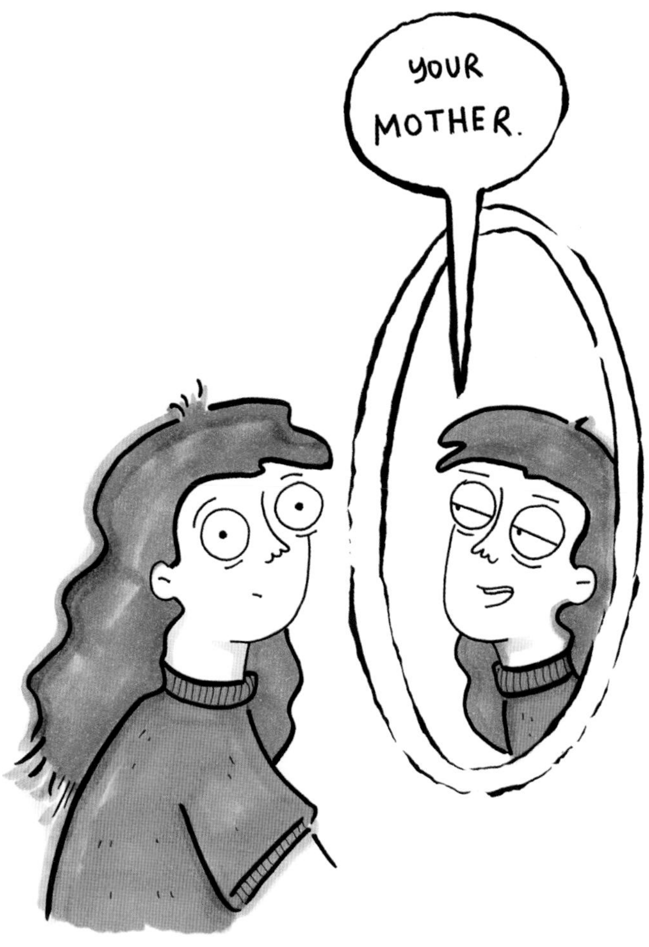
YOUR MOTHER.

WORKING FROM HOME

FIRST,

I NEED
SOME
COFFEE

... AND
A
SNACK

AND AN
INTERESTING
PODCAST

SUGGESTED FOR YOU

MY SECOND-FAVORITE TRUE CRIMES

STUFF YOU WISH YOU DIDN'T KNOW

HMMM... MAYBE SOMETHING NEW TODAY ...

WRITE "TO DO" LIST

1
2
3

I SHOULD STAY HYDRATED.

WONDER WHAT'S ON INSTAGRAM.

NOW I HAVE TO PEE.

JUST GONNA LIGHT THIS CANDLE.

STILL NOTHING

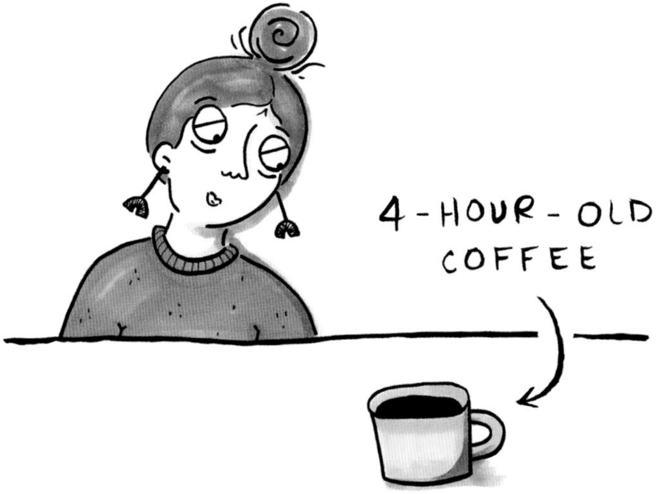
4-HOUR-OLD COFFEE

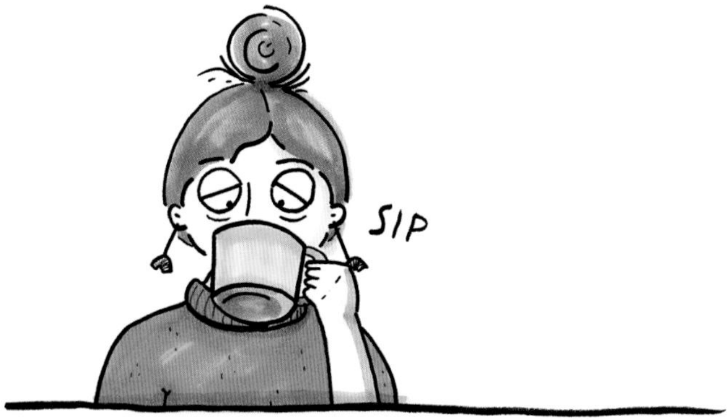
SIP

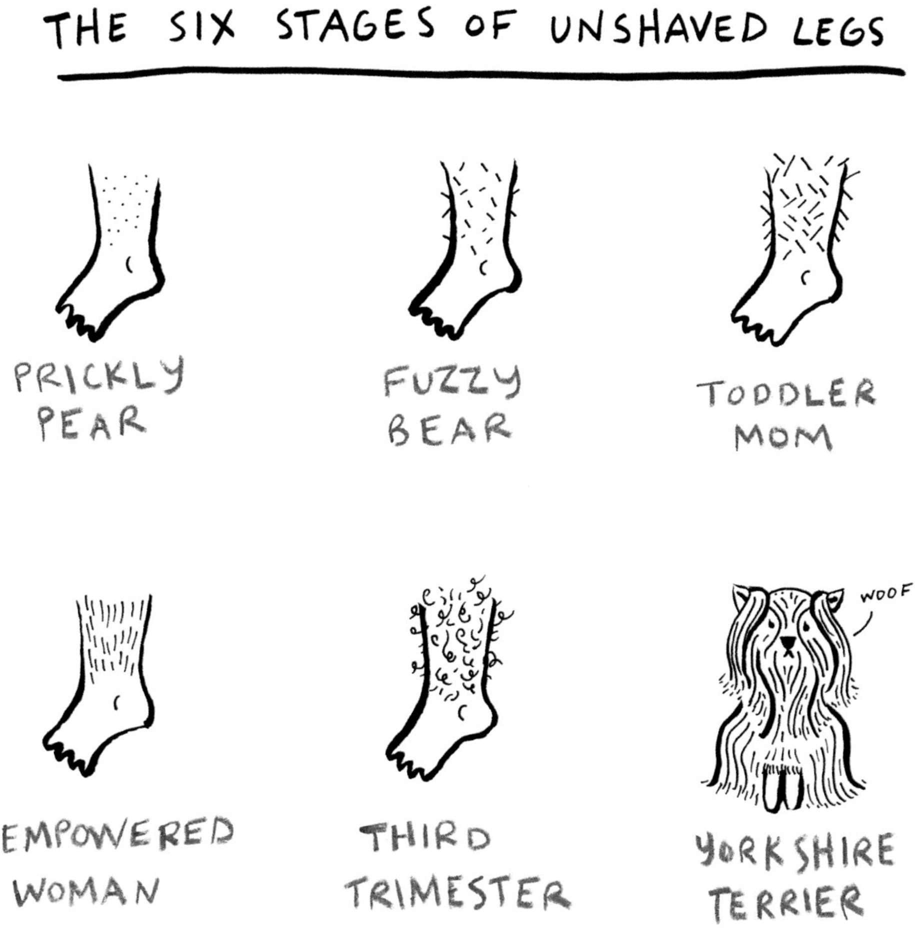
THE SIX STAGES OF UNSHAVED LEGS
PRICKLY PEAR
FUZZY BEAR
TODDLER MOM
EMPOWERED WOMAN
THIRD TRIMESTER
WOOF
YORKSHIRE TERRIER

TIME TO WRITE

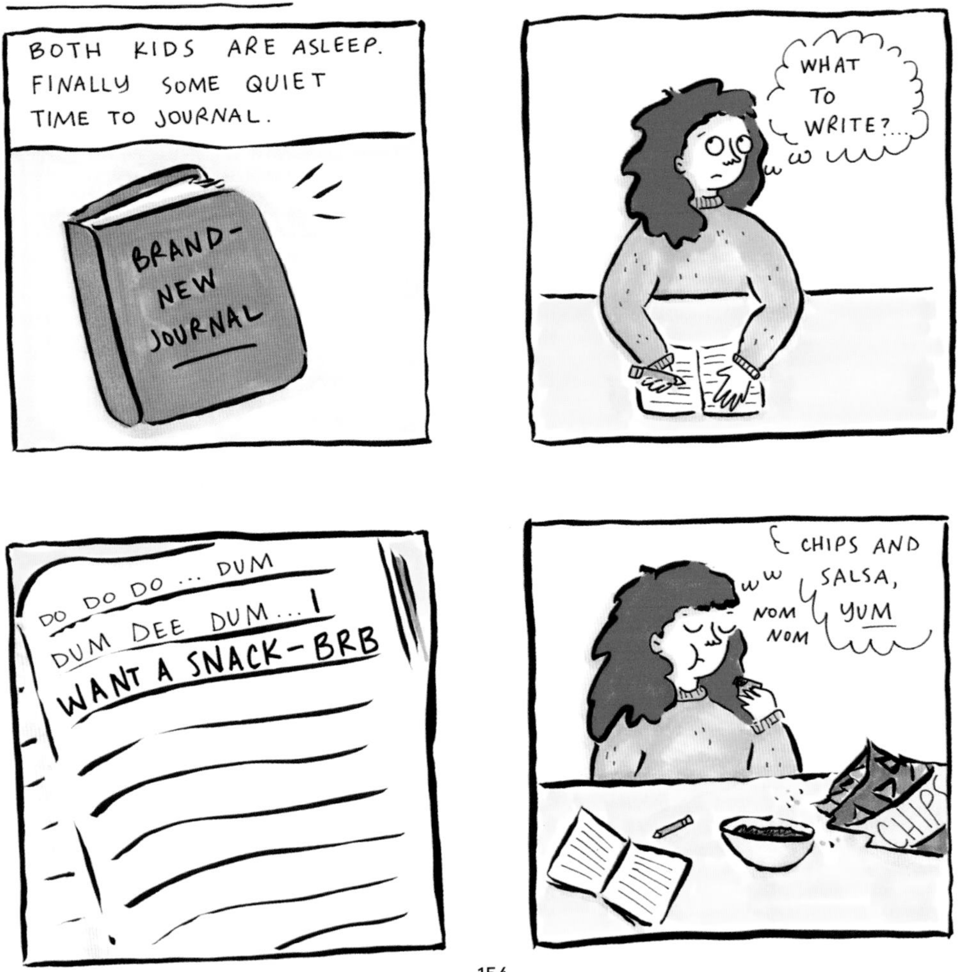
BOTH KIDS ARE ASLEEP. FINALLY SOME QUIET TIME TO JOURNAL.
BRAND-NEW JOURNAL
WHAT TO WRITE?...
DO DO DO ... DUM DUM DEE DUM... I WANT A SNACK-BRB
CHIPS AND SALSA, YUM
NOM NOM
CHIPS

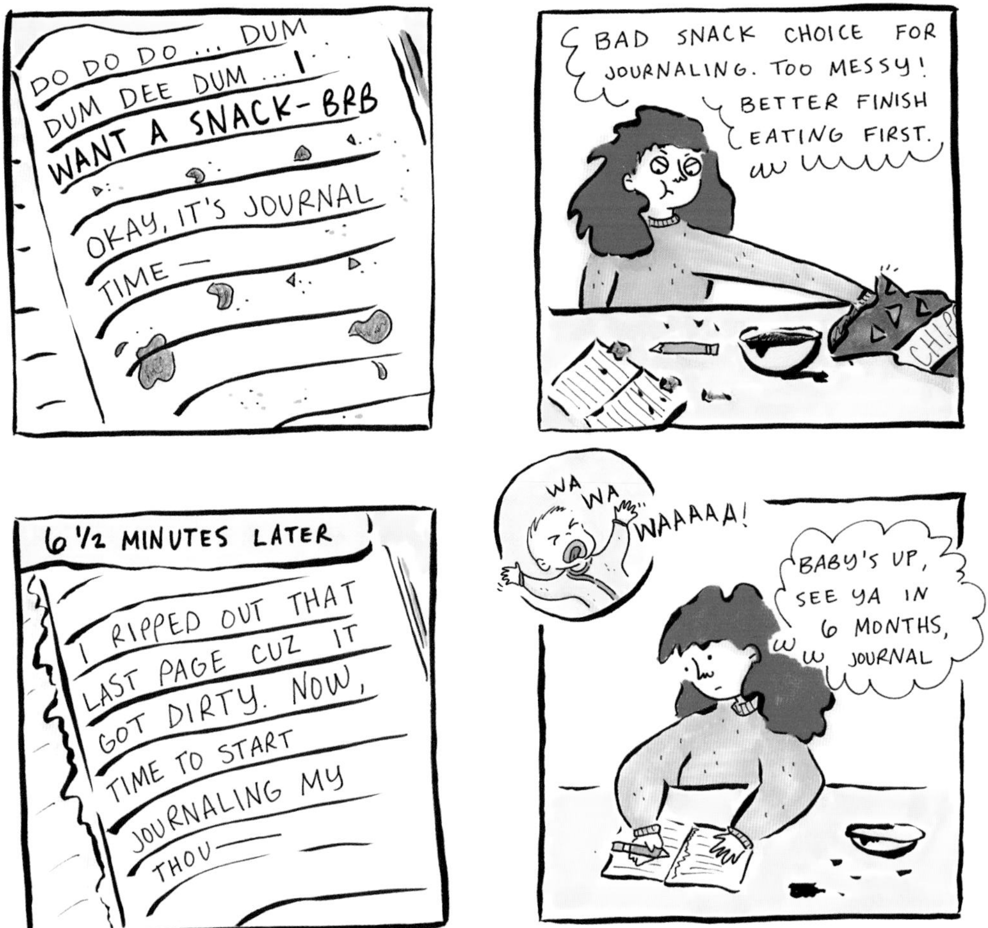
DO DO DO ... DUM
DUM DEE DUM ... I
WANT A SNACK-BRB
OKAY, IT'S JOURNAL
TIME —
BAD SNACK CHOICE FOR JOURNALING. TOO MESSY!
BETTER FINISH EATING FIRST.
CHIPS
6 1/2 MINUTES LATER
I RIPPED OUT THAT
LAST PAGE CUZ IT
GOT DIRTY. NOW,
TIME TO START
JOURNALING MY
THOU—
WA
WA
WAAAAA!
BABY'S UP, SEE YA IN 6 MONTHS, JOURNAL

MORNING SYMPHONY

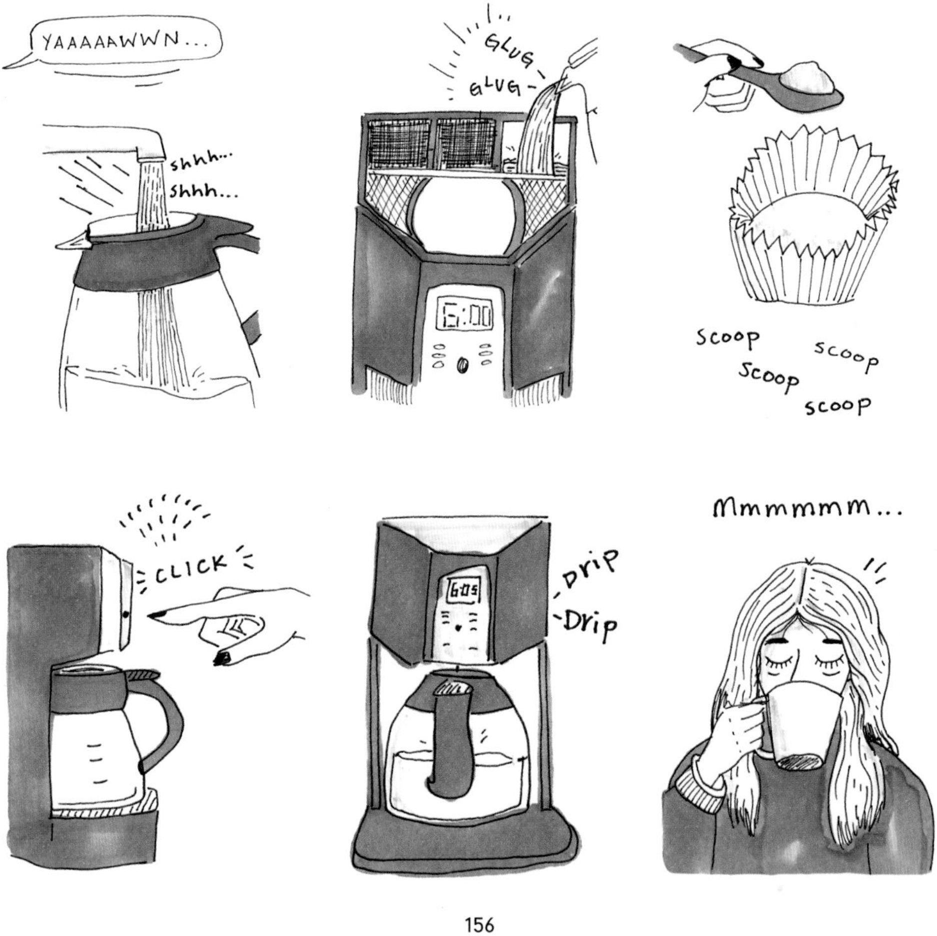
YAAAAAWWN...
shhh...
shhh...
GLUG
GLUG
6:00
scoop
scoop
scoop
scoop
CLICK
6:05
Drip
Drip
Mmmmmm...

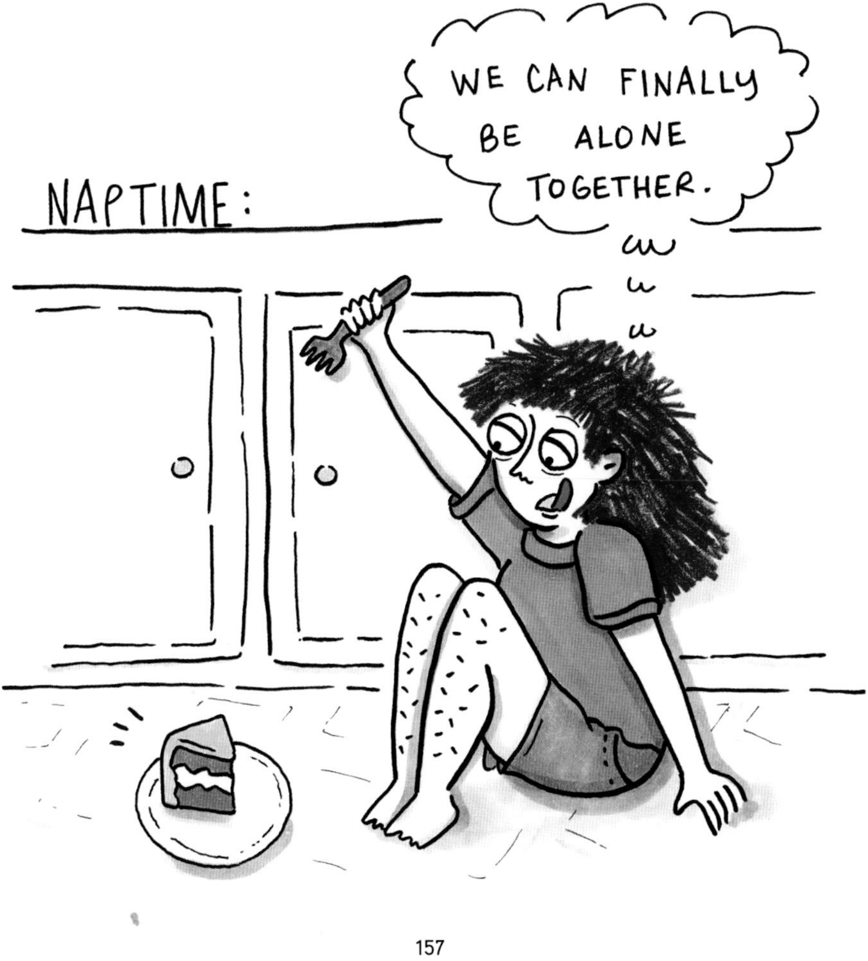
NAPTIME:
WE CAN FINALLY BE ALONE TOGETHER.

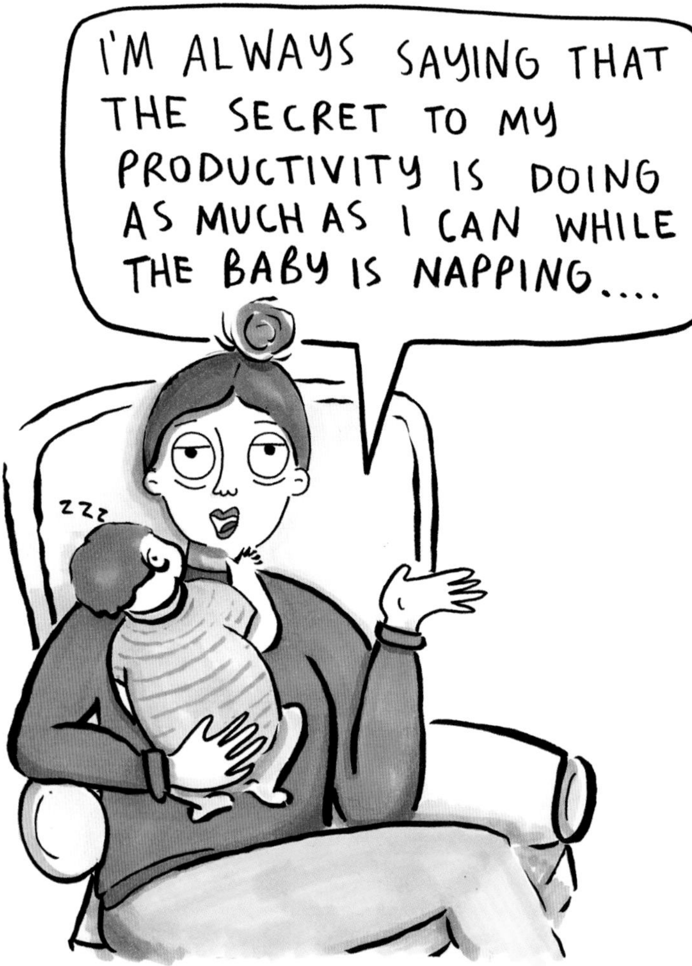
I'M ALWAYS SAYING THAT THE SECRET TO MY PRODUCTIVITY IS DOING AS MUCH AS I CAN WHILE THE BABY IS NAPPING....
ZZZ

8 SECONDS LATER

SLEEPING IN

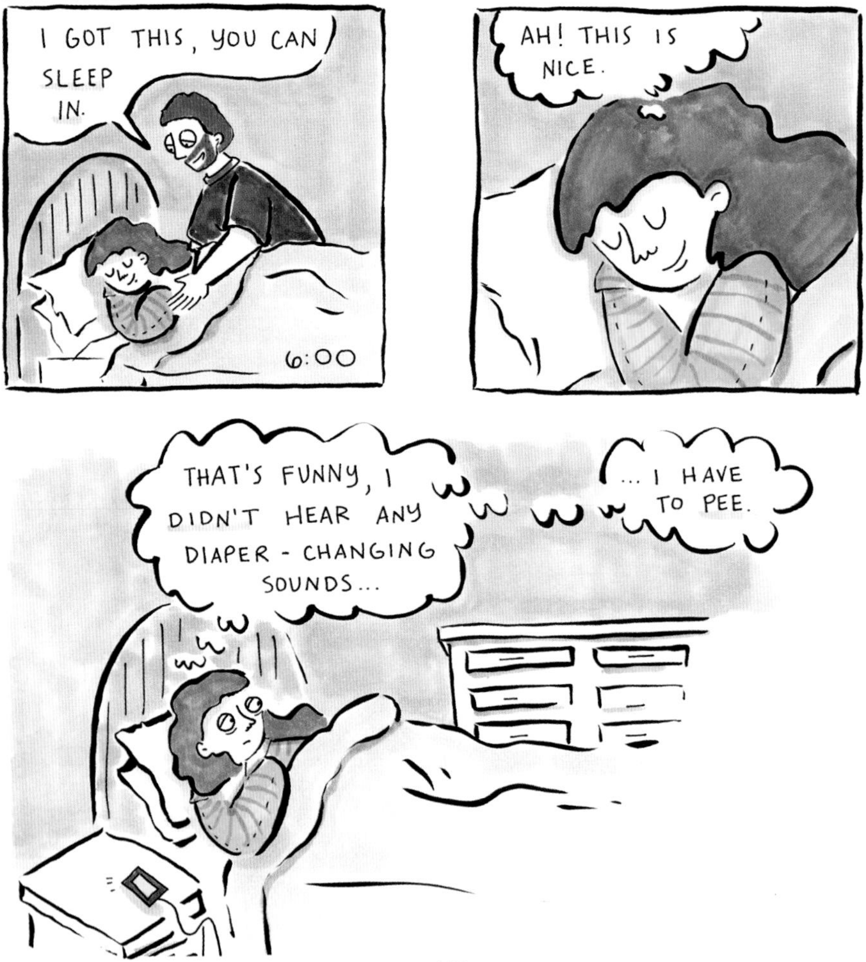
I GOT THIS, YOU CAN SLEEP IN.
6:00
AH! THIS IS NICE.
THAT'S FUNNY, I DIDN'T HEAR ANY DIAPER - CHANGING SOUNDS...
... I HAVE TO PEE.

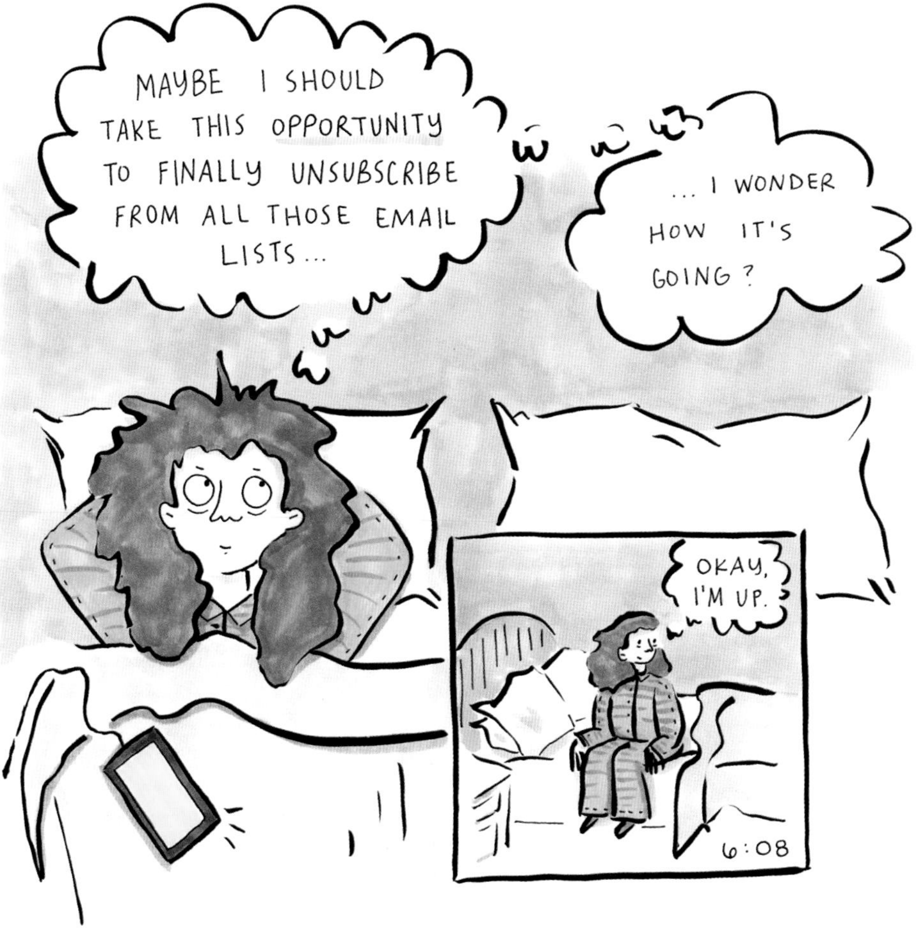
MAYBE I SHOULD TAKE THIS OPPORTUNITY TO FINALLY UNSUBSCRIBE FROM ALL THOSE EMAIL LISTS...
... I WONDER HOW IT'S GOING?
OKAY, I'M UP.
6:08

MY SLEEPING CHAIR

REQUESTING TIME OFF

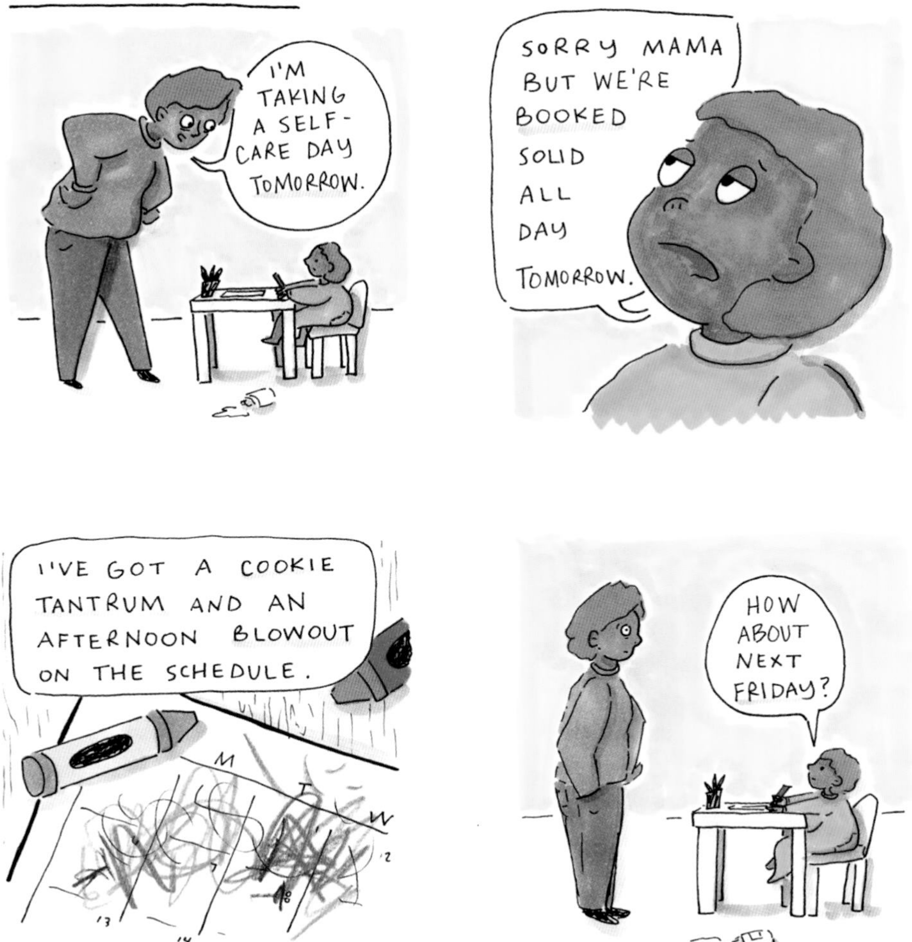
I'M TAKING A SELF-CARE DAY TOMORROW.
SORRY MAMA BUT WE'RE BOOKED SOLID ALL DAY TOMORROW.
I'VE GOT A COOKIE TANTRUM AND AN AFTERNOON BLOWOUT ON THE SCHEDULE.
HOW ABOUT NEXT FRIDAY?

SPIRITUAL

WILL I HAVE TIME TO SHOWER TODAY?

DON'T COUNT ON IT

YOU JUST DON'T PAY ATTENTION TO ME ANYMORE.

TODAY'S CARD IS THE SLEEPY-EYED PEASANT ...AGAIN.

PEASANT

ABCDEFGHIJKLM NOPQRS TUVWXYZ
1 2 3 4 5 6 7 8 9 0

I MISS

MANI-PEDI

MAMA

THE TEA LEAVES SAY THAT YOU REALLY NEED SOME <u>COFFEE</u>.

THIS IS YOUR BOREDOM LINE ... THAT'S FUNNY, IT LOOKS LIKE IT SUDDENLY STOPPED!

IF YOUR CHEST FEELS TIGHT, THAT'S BECAUSE YOUR FUTURE IS FILLED WITH HUGS.

DO YOU NEED ANY HELP?

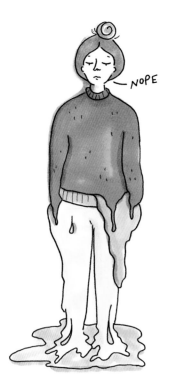

NOPE

YOU SURE?

I'M OKAY...

ANCIENT CONSTELLATIONS

MYTHICAL MEMORIES FROM PRE-MOMMY LIFE

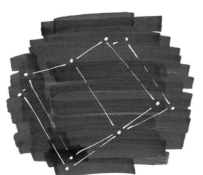

THE BIG READER

BRUNCH HERO

MY SVELTE BELT

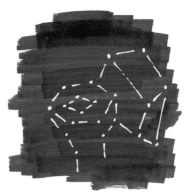

THE THINKER

SOMETIMES I'M LUCKY ENOUGH TO GET AN ENTIRE AFTERNOON TO MYSELF.

LOW BATTERY

WHAT DO I DO WITH MY TEMPORARY FREEDOM?

① GET LOST IN A BOOKSTORE.

② GO SHOPPING FOR OUTFITS I WILL PROBABLY NEVER WEAR.

AND I CAN TRY THEM ALL ON!

③ GRAB A CUP OF COFFEE AND ENJOY THE PEACE AND QUIET OF MY CAR.

NO MATTER WHAT I CHOOSE TO DO ON MY BREAK,

THE BEST PART IS

COMING HOME.

THE END

HOW I MADE THIS BOOK

FILLING A BOOK WITH 160 COMICS WHILE CHASING TWO TODDLERS ALL DAY ISN'T EXACTLY EASY. THE SECRET IS TO TAKE IT ONE MESSY, IMPERFECT STEP AT A TIME.

1 GATHER IDEAS

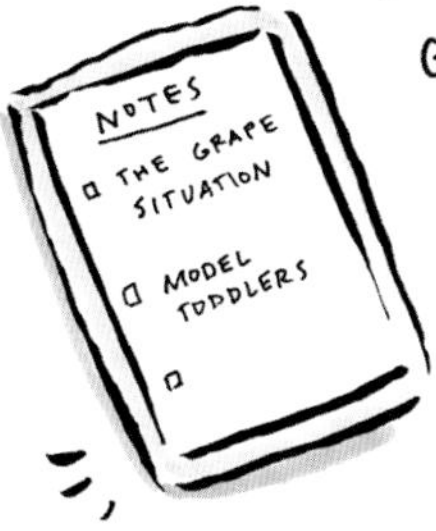
NOTES
THE GRAPE SITUATION
MODEL TODDLERS

I STARTED A GIANT LIST OF IDEAS ON MY PHONE.

I STILL ADD TO IT EVERY DAY.

2 SKETCH

I MADE MOUNTAINS OF HORRIBLE SKETCHES AND KEPT ONLY THE BEST.

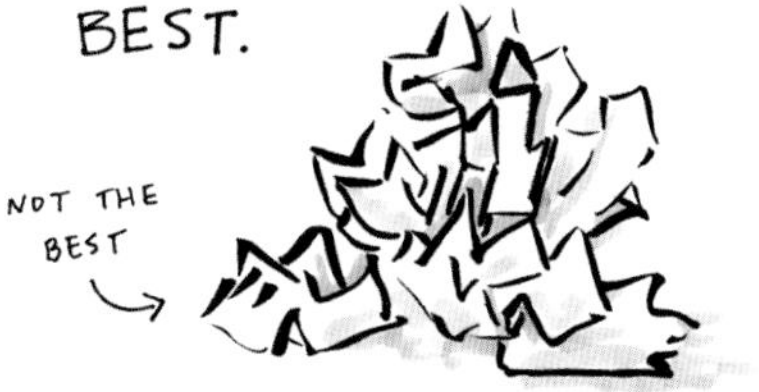
NOT THE BEST

③ CREATE THE FINAL ART

I USED A LIGHTBOX TO HELP TRANSFER THE SKETCHES ONTO A CLEAN SHEET OF SMOOTH BRISTOL.

I USED BRUSH PENS AND FINELINERS FOR THE BLACK LINE WORK.

FINALLY, I ADDED COLORS WITH COPIC MARKERS.

④ SCAN AND EDIT

I SCANNED ALL THE FINAL DRAWINGS AND EDITED EACH ONE ON MY COMPUTER.

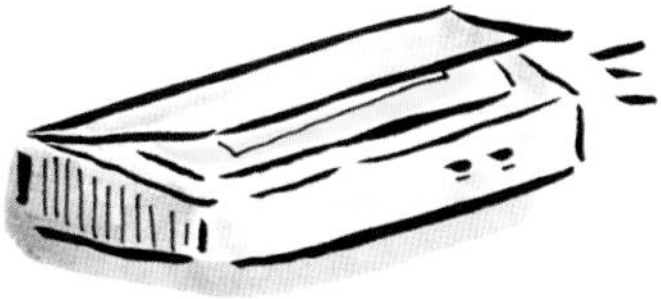

⑤ ADJUST

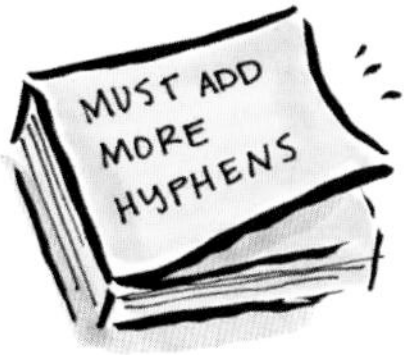
MUST ADD MORE HYPHENS

IN THE FOLLOWING MONTHS, I MADE IMPROVEMENTS BASED ON FEEDBACK.

⑥ BREW COFFEE... SO MUCH COFFEE

THIS STEP IS OPTIONAL BUT VERY HIGHLY RECOMMENDED THROUGHOUT THE ENTIRE PROCESS.

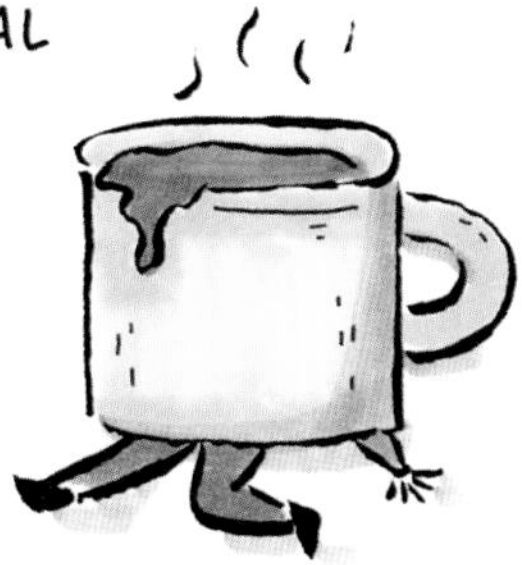

THANK YOU!

- To my husband, Jake, for literally carrying me through this.

- To my editor, Cate Coulacos Prato, for seeing a vision of this book before I did.

- To my agent, Mackenzie Brady Watson, for jumping in and going above and beyond with this one.

- To Mom, Sara, Chris, Kristin, and Promise for countless hours of babysitting so I could draw 160 pages of comics.

- To my online community of moms who provided loads of inspiration and new perspectives on motherhood.

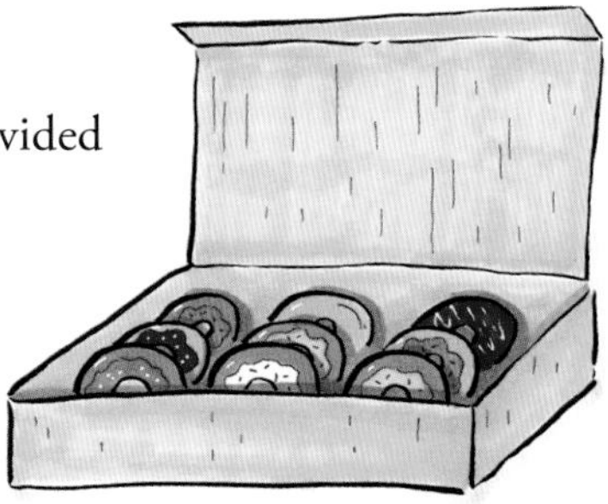

ABOUT THE AUTHOR

Gina McMillen is an artist and teacher living in Phoenix. Since choosing to stay home to raise her two children, Gina has documented the good, the bad, and the hilarious sides of mom life with her comics. Her work is instantly relatable and reminds new and experienced moms that they are not alone. Keep up with Gina's latest comics and projects online at GinaMcMillen.com.